Casseroles & Bakes

SARAH BROWN
A committed vegetarian, yet refreshingly undoctrinaire in her approach, Sarah Brown believes in eating good healthy food and in eating well. She gives regular demonstrations and lectures, and, as national coordinator of cookery for the Vegetarian Society of the United Kingdom, runs a series of cookery courses. Well known for her highly successful BBC television series "Vegetarian Kitchen" and for her bestselling "Sarah Brown's Vegetarian Cookbook" and "Sarah Brown's Healthy Living Cookbook", she has played a major role in promoting public awareness of the link between health and diet and the widespread move towards a healthier style of eating.

CHRISTINE SMITH
Christine Smith has been a vegetarian for ten years. Her early experience of helping to run a small wholefood shop later led her to develop a vegetarian catering business, supplying fresh and frozen wholefood. She now gives regular talks and demonstrations on vegetarian cookery in East Anglia, where she lives, and is a qualified teacher of the Vegetarian Society's Cordon Vert diploma courses. She also appears frequently on local radio and contributes articles and recipes to a number of magazines.

SAINSBURY'S
HEALTHY·EATING
·COOKBOOKS·

Casseroles & Bakes

CHRISTINE SMITH

SERIES·EDITOR
SARAH BROWN

CONTENTS

Casseroles & Bakes was conceived, edited and designed by Dorling Kindersley Limited, 9 Henrietta Street, London WC2E 8PS

Published exclusively for J Sainsbury plc, Stamford House, Stamford Street, London SE1 9LL
by Dorling Kindersley Limited, 9 Henrietta Street, London WC2E 8PS

First published 1986

Copyright © 1986 by Dorling Kindersley Limited, London   Text copyright © 1986 by Sarah Elizabeth Brown Limited
Recipes by Christine Smith

ISBN 0-86318-146-5

Printed in Italy

INTRODUCTION

*Colourful, tasty and nutritious, the recipes in this book offer an exciting
range of main courses, side dishes and desserts. Through the use of
wholesome ingredients and by careful cooking, you can create vegetarian
meals that are delicious, easy, and very healthy.*

HOW CASSEROLES CAN BE HEALTHY

These dishes contain plenty of fresh vegetables and fruits; unrefined grains, such as wholemeal flour, pasta and brown rice; nuts and seeds; beans and lentils; and are therefore rich in minerals, vitamins, fibre and high quality protein. The recipes use oils that are high in polyunsaturated fat; and dairy products that are low in fat and calories but rich in calcium and protein, such as skimmed milk and low-fat yogurt.

Pulses are very useful in a healthy vegetarian diet. Filling, rich in protein and low in fat, they are versatile, adaptable and absorb flavours extremely well. People often worry that a meatless diet will be lacking in protein, but the combinations in many of these casseroles, such as pulses and grains, nuts and grains, grains and dairy products, will provide excellent amounts of complete proteins in a very acceptable form.

MAKING THE MOST OF CASSEROLES AND BAKES

The range of ingredients used in this book are full of colour, flavour, texture and goodness. Used with imagination, they turn a simple dish into an exciting and original meal. Always select and prepare vegetables and fruit with care (see p.8) and be gentle when cooking them. To retain the maximum nutrients, use the minimum of oil; steam rather than boil and bake rather than fry.

How you flavour a dish and the accompaniments you choose are important. There are many ways of seasoning a dish with natural ingredients. You do not have to rely on salt – there are better, more healthy ways of enhancing the flavours (see pp. 18–19) and a vast array of herbs and spices,

both fresh and dried, are available. Increase your range gradually and discover the distinctive flavours that each creates. Sweeteners like concentrated fruit juices and dried fruits can be used in dessert recipes to create tangy natural flavours without the harmful effects of sugar (see p. 8).

The vegetable or sauce that accompanies a casserole should be chosen to complement and contrast in texture, flavour and colour. A moist bean casserole, for example, would combine well with a lightly steamed green vegetable like broccoli, and a bright carrot and orange salad would enhance a substantial nut loaf with a creamy sauce.

WHAT IS A HEALTHY DIET?

There now seems little question that good health is dependent on a healthy diet, no smoking and plenty of exercise. But what is a healthy diet? There seem to be a bewildering number of

conflicting answers against a background of tempting new products, all advertised as "natural", "healthy" and "wholesome". What are the real facts?

FOOD FASHIONS

With the development of nutritional science over the last 100 years, the major nutrients – protein, fat, carbohydrate, vitamins and minerals – appear to have fallen in and out of favour. Shortly after the war, everyone was urged to eat more protein, but today we are told that the Western world consumes too much of this expensive energy source. Recently there has been a well-publicized debate about fats: is margarine better for you than butter? Carbohydrate, once the enemy of the slimming industry is now back in favour, as a result of the pro-fibre campaign. Yet sugar, another carbohydrate, has been blamed for tooth decay, obesity and adult-onset diabetes. Each of these fashions spawn a new "diet", which in turn encourages unbalanced eating.

GETTING THE BALANCE RIGHT

All the major nutrients have distinctive and important roles to play in our diet, and it is now clear that a healthy diet means eating not only the right quantity, but also the right type of each one (see pp.90–93).

The Western diet is very high in fat, sugar and salt, and low in fibre, fresh fruit and vegetables. The guidelines for a healthy diet, summed up by the reports prepared by the National Advisory Committee on Nutrition Education and the Committee on Medical Aspects of Food Policy are:

• Eat more unrefined carbohydrates which contain fibre (see pp.90–92).

• Eat more fresh fruit and vegetables, which contain fibre as well as vitamins and minerals.

• Eat less fat, sugar and salt (see pp. 90–92).

Adopting a healthy diet that will positively help your long- and short-term health is, therefore, only a shift of emphasis, which can quickly become a way of life.

WHAT IS WRONG WITH A HIGH-FAT DIET?

High-fat diets have been clearly linked with incidence of coronary heart disease. Moreover, a high-fat diet tends to be a low-fibre diet, which is associated with intestinal disorders, constipation, diverticulitis and cancer of the colon. One further danger – on a high-fat diet, it is easy to consume excess calories, as fat contains more than twice the number of calories, weight for weight, as carbohydrate and protein. Surplus fat is stored in the body as fatty deposits, which can lead to obesity and its attendant problems of diabetes, high blood pressure and gall bladder disease. It is important to cut down your fat intake to about 30–35 per cent of the day's calories or less. There are three types of fat, which need to be distinguished according to their origin and their interaction with cholesterol.

SATURATED FATS
Mainly found in foods from animal sources (particularly red meat fat, full-fat cheeses, butter and cream), saturated fats are high in cholesterol and if they are eaten in excess, the cholesterol can be laid down as fatty deposits in the blood vessels which can lead to heart disease and atherosclerosis.

POLYUNSATURATED FATS
These fats are mainly found in foods from vegetable sources in liquid oil form usually from plant seeds, such as sunflower and safflower. They are, however, also present in solid form in grains and nuts. Although they contribute to the overall fat intake, they can lower levels of cholesterol in the blood.

MONOUNSATURATED FATS

These fats, which are found in olive oil, have no effect on cholesterol levels, but do add to daily fat intake.

The three types of fat are present in varying proportions in high-fat foods. The fat in butter, for example, contains 63 per cent saturated fat and only 3 per cent polyunsaturated, whereas the fat in polyunsaturated margarine contains 65 per cent polyunsaturated and 12 per cent saturated fat.

WHAT IS WRONG WITH A SUGAR-RICH DIET?

Sugar, or sucrose, in the form of refined white or brown sugar is all too easy to eat, but contributes only calories to a diet. Sugar not used immediately for fuel is converted into fat, encouraging weight gain. Sugar is also a principle factor in tooth decay. Highly refined carbohydrates, particularly sugar are also absorbed easily into the bloodstream, quickly increasing blood sugar levels. If the body overreacts to this, the blood sugar levels drop dramatically, leaving the desire to eat something sweet and thus creating a vicious circle. In addition, the cells that produce insulin cannot always cope with sudden concentrations of glucose and diabetes may result. Try not only to cut down on sugar in drinks and cooking, but when cutting down, take particular care to avoid manufactured foods, both sweet and savoury, where sugar comes near the top of the list of ingredients. Always check the nutritional labelling on the container.

WHY DO WE NEED LESS SALT?

There is a clear link in certain people between salt intakes and high blood pressure – a condition that can lead to circulatory problems, such as heart disease and strokes. The sodium from salt works with potassium in regulating body fluids. Excess salt upsets this balance, which puts a strain on the kidneys. In general, we eat more salt than we need. Do be aware of the amount hidden in processed foods and try not to add more during home cooking.

WHAT IS SO GOOD ABOUT FIBRE?

High-fibre foods are more filling than other foods, take longer to chew and satisfy hunger for longer, which reduces the temptation to eat between meals. They are also less completely digested, thus helping to reduce actual calorie intake. The evidence strongly suggests that lack of dietary fibre can cause cancer of the colon in addition to simple constipation. A low-fibre diet often means a high-fat, high-sugar diet with the problems that induces, including adult-onset diabetes. Only plant foods, in the form of unrefined carbohydrates, like whole grains and fresh fruit and vegetables, contain fibre and it is critical to eat more. Simply switching to high-fibre breakfast cereals, from refined flours and pastas to wholemeal, in addition to eating plenty of fresh fruit and vegetables will dramatically increase your fibre intake.

Christine Smith

Sarah Brown

USING WHOLEFOODS

The first step in a healthy diet is to choose fresh and wholefoods that are unrefined and as close to their natural state as possible. Simply buy plenty of fresh fruit and vegetables, and use wholemeal flour, bread, pasta and pastry and health foods and whole grains, such as beans and oatmeal. When buying convenience food, select those that contain natural ingredients and the minimum of artificial colours, flavourings and preservatives. These steps alone will ensure that your diet is high in unrefined carbohydrate, rich in vitamins and minerals and lower in fat, salt and sugar.

USING THIS BOOK

The aim of this book is to translate the simple rules for health into a practical and enjoyable form. The recipes are naturally low in fat, high in fibre and unrefined ingredients, with natural sweeteners replacing sugar. Ingredients are used in their most nutritious form.

Healthy eating is not boring, nor does it involve a sacrifice. It is simply a matter of choosing and using more nutritious foods to create delicious, yet healthy meals.

HOW TO STORE AND PREPARE VEGETABLES

● Buy as fresh as possible, keep in a cool, dark place. Do not store in polythene.

● Eat green vegetables as soon as possible after purchase: courgettes, aubergines, mushrooms and peppers will keep for about 1 week in the fridge.

● Keep carrots, potatoes and onions in cool conditions for up to 3 weeks.

● Do not prepare vegetables too far in advance as the cut surface will cause vitamin loss.

● Only peel when absolutely necessary as valuable nutrients lie just beneath the surface and are lost in the process. But scrub well to remove dirt or chemicals.

● Use the minimum amount of oil when frying; steam rather than boil; grill or bake rather than fry; liquidize rather than sieve – these steps all ensure that the maximum nutrients are retained.

HOW TO STORE PULSES

● Store dried pulses in a cool, dry place and use within 6–9 months. Do not use if they look shrivelled.

● Store cooked pulses for up to 5 days in the fridge.

HOW TO STORE NUTS AND SEEDS

● Store nuts in their shells where possible; they will keep for 6 months if kept cool.

● Keep seeds and shelled nuts in an airtight container for up to 3 months. They will go rancid quickly if left in a warm place.

● Use ready-prepared nuts in 4–6 weeks. Use the date mark on the packet as a guide.

HOW TO STORE AND PREPARE DRIED FRUIT

● Keep dried fruit for up to a year in an airtight container, but preferably use within 6 months. Citrus peel in the container will keep fruit moist.

● Dried fruit will keep frozen for a year; reconstituted, it will keep frozen for 2–3 months.

● Plump up dried fruit by soaking for 8–12 hours in fresh water, cold tea or fruit juice. Or simmer, covered, for 10–15 minutes, then leave to stand for 1 hour.

HOW TO COOK PULSES

Soak pulses for 8–12 hours before cooking. Drain and bring to the boil in plenty of fresh, unsalted water. Boil fast for 10 minutes to remove toxins, remove any scum from the surface, then cover and cook as follows:

35 mins	50 mins	Other
Aduki	Black beans	Split peas*
Black-eyed	Butter (lima)	Lentils*
Cannellini	Haricot	Soya beans**
Flageolet	Pinto	
Red kidney	Chick peas	
	Green peas	

* Split peas and lentils do not need soaking or fast boiling. Cook whole lentils for 30–45 minutes; split lentils for 15–30 minutes; split peas for 40–45 minutes.

** Soya beans need to fast boil for a whole hour and then cook for a further 1–1½ hours.

Alternatively, if you are short of time, give the beans a short, hot soak. Cover with plenty of cold water, bring to the boil, simmer for 2–3 minutes. Remove from the heat, cover and leave to stand for 1 hour. Drain and bring to the boil in plenty of fresh, unsalted water. Boil fast for 10 minutes, then cover the pan and cook as follows.

INGREDIENTS

Part of the joy of cooking is choosing the ingredients – especially when this involves selecting fresh fruit, herbs and vegetables and trying out new, unusual and exotic foods.

Always buy the freshest ingredients possible – they contain more vitamins and minerals and have a much better flavour and texture than preserved foods. Grains, pulses, flours, cereals and dried fruit, herbs and spices, however, generally keep for at least 3 months, so it is worth maintaining a small store of basic dry ingredients, particularly those that need to be soaked or cooked in advance. It is also useful to keep a small selection of canned or bottled fruit, vegetables and beans for emergencies. But try to select those without artificial additives or a high sugar or salt content and use them by the "best before" date.

The range of "healthy" ingredients has grown dramatically in recent years, particularly low-fat, reduced sugar, reduced salt, high fibre and vegetarian alternatives to traditional foods. These open the way to both a healthier and a more varied diet and offer endless possibilities for personal variations. The success of a recipe depends as much on the quality of the raw materials as on the way you combine them. In many cases, it is better to use a fresh alternative than to use the specified ingredient if it is not at its best – use fresh, ripe peaches, for example, in place of hard or over-ripe nectarines.

The following pages illustrate many of the familiar and the unusual ingredients found in the recipes in this book – from staples, to flavourings and dairy products. The section acts as both an identification guide and a reference source. You will find advice on choosing and storing food, together with useful information about the origins, culinary applications and nutritional value of specific ingredients. For more detailed nutritional information, see pages 90–93.

LEAVES ^{AND} ROOTS

Vegetables are a good source of vitamins and minerals and are generally low in carbohydrates and fats. All roots, except celeriac, should be scrubbed, not peeled, as most nutrients are just under the skin. If necessary, store vegetables in a cool, dark place and prepare as simply and quickly as possible, since light, water and air reduce the nutrient content, particularly Vitamins B_1, B_{12} and C, and iodine.

WATERCRESS

High in minerals, especially iodine, this nutritious leaf with its clean peppery taste is excellent in stir-fries, soups, salads and as a garnish.

TURNIPS

The green-leafed tops are used as a leaf vegetable and the mineral-rich root in soups and casseroles. They contain some Vitamin C.

CELERIAC

This vegetable looks like a turnip and tastes a little like celery. A good source of fibre, it combines well with potatoes and is good in stews and soups.

KOHLRABI

A member of the cabbage family, and used in the same way as turnips. Weight for weight, a kohlrabi contains more Vitamin C than an orange.

BEETROOT

Beetroot's brilliant purple colour makes it popular in salads and soups. It is a source of folic acid, minerals and Vitamin C and is often pickled in vinegar.

GARLIC

A member of the lily family, probably from Asia, garlic can enhance any savoury dish or dressing.

RED CABBAGE

Use it in pies, salads and roasts, but always cook in lemon juice or vinegar to prevent it turning blue.

SHALLOTS

These subtle-tasting young onions are excellent in salads, casseroles and pies.

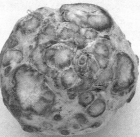

BLACK OLIVES

Olives are high in minerals and polyunsaturated fat, low in vitamins and contain some fibre.

SPINACH

An excellent source of Vitamin A, calcium and iron, spinach is delicious with eggs or in soups, bakes and salads. Sorrel is similar in appearance and taste.

GARDEN CRESS

Usually grown and eaten with mustard, cress is a sprout at the two leaf stage. It is high in Vitamins A and C and good in salads, soups and sandwiches.

LEEKS

A winter vegetable from the onion family, but with a subtler taste. Also known as "poor man's asparagus", leeks are suitable for casseroles, soups, stews and gratins. They contain Vitamin B_6 and iron.

PARSNIPS

A winter root vegetable that resembles the sweet potato. The sweetish taste makes it suitable for curries, purées and glazed desserts.

CHINESE LEAVES

This crisp, delicate vegetable is delicious in salads, stir-fries and bakes.

FRUIT ᴬᴺᴰ VEGETABLES

Fresh fruit and vegetables are important in casseroles and bakes as they contribute colour to the appearance of a dish and moisture to the texture. They are also valuable for their fibre and vitamin content.

PEPPERS

Peppers, red, green and yellow, have a slightly sweet taste which goes well with grains and pasta. They are available all year, fresh and canned.

MANGETOUT

A variety of pea with an edible pod, mangetout are a rich source of fibre. A good side vegetable, they also combine well with rice.

TOMATOES

Tomatoes, available all year round, provide a flavour, colour and texture which complements other ingredients.

MUSHROOMS

There are many varieties, including field, button and open mushrooms (below). They are all slightly different in texture, flavour and shape.

PINEAPPLE

Pineapple is a tropical fruit, available all year round. It stores well and can be bought fresh or canned.

PEARS

Dessert pears are rich in fibre. Their sweet, white flesh is delicious casseroled with other fruit or vegetables. Use quickly as they deteriorate rapidly.

PEACHES

Fresh peaches have a very short season, but are also available canned and dried. Store fresh peaches in a cool, dark place.

BLACK GRAPES

There are two main types of grape – wine-making and dessert grapes, both available at all times of year and both delicious raw. There is little difference in taste between the white and black varieties.

FRENCH BEANS

French beans are a member
of the large runner bean
family and need topping
and tailing before cooking.

RUNNER BEANS

Runner beans must be topped, tailed
and stripped of tough strings before
cooking.

BROCCOLI

Broccoli is a variety of cauliflower. It is rich
in Vitamin C, makes an excellent side dish
and combines well with nuts in light
casseroles.

OKRA

Okra can be used to thicken or
flavour casseroles. Eat raw
or cooked.

FENNEL

Fennel's clean, fresh flavour
lends sharpness to a dish. It can
be eaten raw or cooked and
complements cheese.

SWEETCORN

Sweetcorn, available fresh,
frozen and canned, is a rich
source of fibre, and
excellent in casseroles
and bakes.

CELERY

Celery can be bought all year
round and is sold fresh and
canned. Store celery in an
airtight container in the fridge,
but use as quickly as possible.

CAULIFLOWER

Cauliflower is a member of the cabbage
family, available all year round.

BEANS ~ LENTILS

Beans and lentils provide the staple food of millions throughout the world. All beans are rich in protein and when combined with grains, flours, nuts, seeds or dairy produce they provide a very high-quality protein. Most are also rich in fibre, vitamins and minerals. All pulses are readily available dried and many beans are also sold pre-cooked in cans. All dried beans should be soaked for 8–12 hours and should be boiled fast for at least 10 minutes before simmering.

GREEN SPLIT PEAS

Split peas are generally sweeter than whole ones. They contain fibre and Vitamins B_1 and B_2 and are delicious in soups, casseroles and bakes.

RED SPLIT LENTILS

These small, orange lentils are a staple food throughout the Middle East, often served with rice. They cook to a purée, do not require soaking, and contain Vitamin B_6, iron, fibre, phosphorus and zinc.

GREEN SPLIT LENTILS

These large, green lentils are an important part of Indian cooking, as a main or side dish with curry. Like split peas they do not require soaking, and contain Vitamin B_6, iron, phosphorus and zinc.

PINTO BEANS

A variety of haricot bean, these lose their colour but not their flavour when cooked. Originally used in spicy Mexican dishes and good in vegetable casseroles and bakes.

LE PUY LENTILS

These small, dark lentils with speckles do not require soaking. Delicious in gratins, casseroles and bakes, they contain Vitamin B_6, iron, fibre, phosphorus and zinc.

ADUKI BEANS

This "Prince of beans" from the Far East has a sweet, strong flavour and is high in protein and fibre. Good in casseroles, loaves and desserts.

BLACK-EYED BEANS

A tender bean that absorbs other flavours well; ideal for bakes, soups and casseroles.

YELLOW SPLIT PEAS

Split peas, like lentils, do not require soaking, and are ideal as a base for soups and casseroles. They contain fibre and Vitamins B_1 and B_2.

BLACK KIDNEY BEANS

Particularly popular throughout Spain and Central and South America, their sweet taste is delicious in soups and casseroles, especially with cumin, bay leaf, tomatoes and garlic. They contain iron.

CHICK PEAS

Chick peas rival lean meat as a source of protein and contain more calcium than any other bean. A staple food in the Middle East, they have a good balance of amino acids, several minerals and some Vitamin C.

MUNG BEANS

Mung beans are popular for sprouting because of their sweet taste and high vitamin content, which when sprouted can increase by 600 per cent, especially C and B Vitamins. Vitamin E is also present.

HARICOT BEANS

These plump, tender beans contain iron, magnesium and zinc. They can be served in casseroles, purées and salads, and are the original baked bean from Boston.

BUTTER BEANS

These slightly floury beans are very popular in casseroles, bakes, loaves, salads and purées. A smaller, sweeter relative is the lima bean.

RED KIDNEY BEANS

With their floury texture and sweet taste these beans are ideal in spicy loaves, roasts and bakes.

GRAINS, NUTS ~ SEEDS

Grains, nuts and seeds have been used from earliest times as rich sources of oil, minerals, vitamins, protein and complex carbohydrates. Grains, an excellent replacement for meat, are readily available cracked, whole, flaked or ground. Nuts come whole, shelled, flaked, nibbed, ground or milled. Seeds can be whole, shelled or roasted. Use unsalted nuts or seeds for cooking.

MILLET

A gluten-free grain with a similar nutrition content to other cereals.

CORNMEAL

This gluten-free flour from maize (corn-on-the-cob) is used as a thickening agent, or with high-gluten flours for bread. Cornmeal is not to be confused with cornflour which is white corn starch.

POT BARLEY

Pot barley is barley with the outer husks removed, so it retains all the vitamins, minerals and fibre of the grain. The delicious creamy, nutty taste is ideal for bakes and soups.

WHEAT GRAIN

An excellent source of protein, fibre, vitamins and minerals (especially zinc when sprouted), wheat grain is delicious in rissoles.

OATMEAL

A good source of protein, fibre, minerals and B Vitamins and delicious in roasts, rissoles, bakes and puddings.

BUCKWHEAT

This protein-rich plant, traditionally used in blinis (Russian buckwheat pancakes) and usually roasted, is a useful casserole ingredient.

BULGAR WHEAT

Boiled, dried and cracked to varying degrees of coarseness, this wheat can be soaked and used uncooked in bakes, stuffings and baked desserts.

CASHEWS

High-protein and low-fat nuts with good levels of calcium, iron and B-group Vitamins.

SWEET OR SPANISH CHESTNUTS

Rich in carbohydrates, potassium, E and B Vitamins and low in protein, fat and fibre, these nuts are good in purées, stuffings, soups, roasts, bakes and desserts.

WALNUTS

High in fat and a good source of protein, fibre, vitamins and minerals. Generally used in sweet recipes, they are also excellent in salads, stuffings and roasts.

SESAME SEEDS

One of the oldest spices and oil-seed crops, these seeds are also made into tahini and gomashio (a salt substitute) and make an excellent garnish. High in calcium, phosphorus and zinc.

SUNFLOWER SEEDS

An excellent source of E and most B Vitamins, especially B_1 and essential fatty acids. Sunflower seeds are also rich in iron and are used in bakes and garnishes.

LONG-GRAIN BROWN RICE

Brown rice is an unrefined carbohydrate, with all the original bran and nutrients. Long-grain rice is used in salads, curries, casseroles and bakes; short-grain is used in desserts.

WHOLEMEAL MACARONI

Macaroni are small tubes of pasta, boiled and then baked with a sauce. Wholemeal macaroni is a good source of fibre and B Vitamins.

WHOLEMEAL SPAGHETTI

A British product, now successfully sold to the Italians, wholemeal spaghetti is made from durum wheat milled by a special process, so it retains the original nutrients. It can be eaten with a sauce, or baked.

OAT FLAKES

Use these in rissoles, bakes, roasts, muesli and puddings. They are rich in B Vitamins and iron.

ALMONDS

A very popular nut, rich in protein, minerals, vitamins and fibre and low in fat. Best in sauces, stuffings and desserts.

HAZELNUTS

Lower in fat than most other nuts, rich in Vitamin E and a good source of protein, this nut is good toasted, in stuffings, salads and roasts.

WHOLEMEAL LASAGNE

Lasagne, flat strips of pasta, is layered with a sauce and then baked. The grain's original nutrients are retained.

HERBS AND SPICES

Herbs and spices should enhance and reinforce the character of a dish, not overpower it. Herbs should usually be used fresh, though oregano, dill, sage, marjoram and bay leaf keep well. To dry herbs, pick before flowering and hang upside down somewhere cool and dark. When dry, crumble and store in airtight containers. Spices should be bought whole.

CARAWAY SEEDS

A pungent spice, native to Europe and Asia. Used to flavour soups, casseroles, vegetables and cheeses.

DILL WEED

A subtly aromatic taste, well-suited to mild foods such as potatoes.

DILL SEEDS

More pungent than dill weed, they combine well with starchy foods, also enhancing their flavour.

CUMIN

The seeds are pungent and savoury, the herb milder. Both are used extensively in curries and spicy casseroles.

THYME

An ingredient of bouquet garni and good with vegetable bakes and casseroles.

BLUE POPPY SEEDS

A mild spice, usually used to decorate or fill bread and confectionery, but also to spice rice dishes.

ROOT GINGER

This spice comes from the rhizome of the Southeast Asian plant. Rich in minerals, it is grated and used in baking and sweet and sour casseroles.

MARJORAM

A fragrant herb, both dried and fresh.

CAPERS

The unopened buds of a Mediterranean shrub which are pickled to enhance the slightly hot aniseed flavour.

BASIL

A strong, pungent herb for casseroles and all pasta.

CORIANDER

The seeds are very aromatic; the leaves are generally used for garnishes.

ROSEMARY

Fresh or dried, the flavour complements beans and vegetables.

PAPRIKA

This mildly hot, sweet spice comes from the ground seeds of pimiento, and is good with goulashes and sauces.

CAYENNE PEPPER

The name covers a wide range of seeds from the capsicum family. Very pungent, so use sparingly in curries and casseroles.

BAY LEAF

Leaf of the Mediterranean sweet bay tree and an ingredient of bouquet garni. Used as a single leaf, it must be removed before serving.

CHILLI

Hotter than paprika and extensively used in curries and any dish in need of some bite.

GARAM MASALA

The name means "hot mixture" and this can be bought or made from cinnamon, cloves, cumin seeds, cardamoms and mace.

CHERVIL

Best used fresh and added just before serving as cooking diminishes the taste. Ideal with finely textured food.

MUSTARD SEEDS

Black seeds are strongest; the white are used as a spice, as the basis to commercial mustards and as a flavouring, for example in pickles.

CHIVES

Subtler tasting and more digestible than onions, they lose their taste when dried, unless freeze-dried. Add to food at the end of cooking.

MINT

There are many different species of mint; apple mint is excellent for cooking.

OREGANO

The wild form of marjoram, very popular in Italy, especially with tomatoes, cheese and beans.

PARSLEY

One of the herbs in bouquet garni and rich in vitamins, calcium, iron and vital trace elements.

SAGE

An excellent herb to counter richness although it can be overpowering. Use to flavour bean or pea casseroles.

DAIRY PRODUCE, ALTERNATIVES AND ~ FLAVOURINGS

Dairy products and their soya-based alternatives are complete proteins containing all the amino acids, but they are often high in calories and saturated fat. Try to use low-calorie, low-fat versions, such as skimmed milk, soya milk and yogurt, which taste just as good and are now readily available. It is also worth using natural alternatives to sugar and salt, which have the added bonus of providing valuable vitamins and minerals.

TAHINI

A strong, calcium-rich sesame seed dip or sauce.

PEANUT BUTTER

A healthy flavouring for dips, sauces and dressings and full of protein, vitamins and minerals.

SMETANA

A low-fat alternative to cream from skimmed milk and cream.

CONCENTRATED APPLE JUICE

A natural sweetener for desserts and sauces.

SOYA MILK

A high-protein substitute for cow's milk, good in sauces.

SHOYU

A fermented soya bean product, high in B Vitamins.

WHOLEGRAIN MUSTARD

A hot mustard from whole white seeds, white wine, allspice and black pepper.

MISO

A fermented soya bean product and excellent source of vegetable protein. Can be used as a base for soups, sauces, and casseroles.

NATURAL YOGURT

A very good source of high quality protein, Vitamin B_2 and calcium. Easily digestible and ideal as a cream substitute.

COTTAGE CHEESE

Mild low-fat curd cheese made from cooked, skimmed cow's milk. A good source of protein, calcium, Vitamins B_2 and B_{12}.

YEAST EXTRACT

Rich in B Vitamins but very salty, so use sparingly.

FIRM TOFU

A hard-pressed soya bean curd from soya milk. High in protein and low in fat, it is a good base to sweet and savoury dishes.

GOAT'S CHEESE

Mild but tangy, with a good mineral balance.

CREAMED COCONUT

Bought in a block and then grated, this is used in baking, desserts and curries.

BEANS
AND
LENTILS

Beans and lentils combine well with sauces, vegetables and fruit to give a wide range of colours, textures and flavours. When served with pasta, rice or other grains, they also constitute a rich source of protein, as well as a tasty and substantial dish.

ADUKI BEANS
IN A SWEET AND SOUR SAUCE

INGREDIENTS

6oz (175g) aduki beans, soaked
2 tsp (10ml) sunflower oil
1 onion, chopped
1 clove garlic, crushed
1 medium red pepper, deseeded and cut into thin strips
6oz (175g) sweetcorn, fresh, frozen or canned
2 tbsp (30ml) arrowroot
1 tbsp (15ml) shoyu
2 tbsp (30ml) cider vinegar
1 tbsp (15ml) concentrated apple juice or clear honey
2 tbsp (30ml) tomato purée
½ pint (300ml) aduki bean stock

•

NUTRITION PROFILE

This recipe is rich in copper, iron, magnesium, folic acid and Vitamins B₁, B₆, C and E. It is also high in fibre and protein.

• Per portion •
Carbohydrate: 32.3g
Protein: 12.3g **Fibre:** 12.9g
Fat: 3.3g **Calories:** 205

Aduki beans cooked in a tangy sauce make a nutritious, high-fibre meal, especially when served with brown rice or wholemeal noodles.

Preparation time: 20 mins (plus 10–12 hours soaking time)
Cooking time: 10 mins (plus 50 mins for the beans)
Serves 4

METHOD

1. Drain the beans. Place in a pan with plenty of fresh water. Bring to the boil and boil fast for 10 minutes. Reduce the heat, cover and simmer for 35 minutes. Drain reserving the liquid.

2. Heat the oil in a large pan and fry the onion and garlic for 5–8 minutes. Add the cooked beans, red pepper and sweetcorn and cook gently for 2–3 minutes.

3. Mix the arrowroot, shoyu, cider vinegar, concentrated apple juice or honey, tomato purée and 2–3 tbsp (30–45ml) of the bean stock into a smooth paste. Pour over the bean mixture, adding the rest of the bean stock.

4. Bring to the boil, reduce the heat and cook gently for about 5 minutes until the sauce becomes clear and glossy. Cook for a further 5 minutes. Serve hot, garnished with cucumber strips and a sprig of parsley.

Illustrated on page 23

RED AND ORANGE CASSEROLE

INGREDIENTS

8oz (250g) red kidney beans, soaked
2 tsp (10ml) sunflower oil
1 onion, chopped
1 yellow pepper, deseeded and cut
into strips
3 medium carrots, sliced
2 tsp (10ml) ground cinnamon
14oz (400g) can of chopped tomatoes
1/4 pint (150ml) red kidney bean stock
2 tsp (10ml) chopped fresh thyme
1 tsp (5ml) shoyu
grated rind and juice of 2 oranges

•

NUTRITION PROFILE

*This dish is rich in Vitamins A, B$_1$, B$_6$, C
and E, calcium, iron, zinc and folic acid.*

• Per portion •
Carbohydrate: 38.3g
Protein: 16g **Fibre:** 19g
Fat: 3.8g **Calories:** 245

*This colourful high-fibre recipe is made up of an unusual combination of
beans and vegetables, flavoured with oranges. If yellow peppers are not
available, use red or green. Serve with noodles and steamed vegetables.*

Preparation time: 15 mins (plus 10–12 hours soaking time)
Cooking time: 20 mins (plus 50 mins for the beans)
Serves 4

METHOD

1. Drain the beans. Put into a saucepan with fresh water. Bring to
the boil and boil fast for 10 minutes. Reduce the heat, cover and
simmer for 35 minutes. Drain, reserving the stock.

2. Heat the oil in a large pan and fry the onion for 5 minutes. Add
the pepper, carrots and cooked beans and cook for 3–4 minutes.

3. Add the cinnamon, then the tomatoes, bean stock, thyme and
shoyu. Cover and simmer for 20 minutes.

4. Add the orange rind and juice. Season and serve hot.

Illustrated opposite

LENTILS AND COURGETTES
IN HERB SAUCE

INGREDIENTS

6oz (175g) green lentils
2 tsp (10ml) sunflower oil
1 onion, chopped
2 sticks celery, chopped
8oz (250g) courgettes, sliced
4oz (125g) peas
2 tbsp (30ml) soya flour
1/2 pint (300ml) lentil stock
2 tbsp (30ml) chopped fresh parsley
3 tbsp (45ml) chopped fresh mint
2 tsp (10ml) fresh oregano

•

NUTRITION PROFILE

*Rich in iron and magnesium and high in
Vitamins B$_1$ and C.*

• Per portion •
Carbohydrate: 32.3g
Protein: 15.5g **Fibre:** 9.5g
Fat: 4.2g **Calories:** 225

*This light vegetable casserole with its creamy, herb-flavoured sauce is
delicious served with new potatoes and a crisp carrot salad.*

Preparation time: 50 mins   Cooking time: 15 mins
Serves 4

METHOD

1. Wash the lentils, place in a pan with plenty of water, bring to
the boil and simmer for 30 minutes. Drain, reserving the stock.

2. Heat the oil in a pan and fry the onion and celery for 5
minutes. Add the courgettes, peas and cooked lentils. Sprinkle
on the soya flour and cook for 2–3 minutes.

3. Add the lentil stock, stirring well, then the parsley, mint and
oregano and a bay leaf. Cook gently for 15 minutes. Stir in 2 tsp
(10ml) shoyu and 1 tbsp (15ml) of lemon juice. Check the
seasoning. Remove the bay leaf and serve hot.

Illustrated opposite

Clockwise from top left: **Red and orange casserole** (*see above*); **Aduki beans in a sweet and sour sauce** (*see p.21*);
Lentils and courgettes in herb sauce (*see above*).

BUTTER BEANS AU GRATIN

INGREDIENTS

8oz (250g) butter beans, soaked
2 tsp (10ml) sunflower oil
6oz (175g) mushrooms, sliced
2 large leeks, sliced
1 tbsp (15ml) wholemeal flour
1/4 tsp chilli powder
1 tsp (5ml) paprika
1/2 pint (300ml) butter bean stock
2 tsp (10ml) fresh thyme
2 tsp (10ml) fresh sage
1 tsp (5ml) miso or yeast extract
2 tbsp (30ml) medium oatmeal

•

NUTRITION PROFILE

*Rich in copper, magnesium, iron, zinc,
folic acid and Vitamins B_1, B_2 and B_6,
this recipe is also high in fibre and protein
and low in fat.*

• Per portion •
Carbohydrate: 36.8g
Protein: 14.4g **Fibre:** 15.2g
Fat: 4.1g **Calories:** 230

*Serve this satisfying bean casserole with jacket potatoes and steamed
carrots and garnish with thyme. If you cannot find miso (a soya bean
paste), use yeast extract.*

Preparation time: 30 mins (plus 10–12 hours soaking time)
Cooking time: 10 mins (plus 1 hour for the beans)
Serves 4

METHOD

1. Drain the beans, cover with fresh water. Boil fast for 10
minutes. Reduce the heat, cover and simmer for 45–50 minutes.

2. Heat the oil in a large pan and gently fry the mushrooms and
leeks for 10 minutes. Sprinkle the flour, chilli powder and paprika
over the top. Cook for 2–3 minutes. Add the beans, stock, thyme
and sage. Cover and cook gently for 15 minutes.

3. Dissolve the miso or yeast extract in 2 tbsp (30ml) boiling
water. Add to the bean mixture. Check the seasoning, then place
in an ovenproof dish. Sprinkle with the oatmeal. Brown under a
preheated grill. Serve hot.

Illustrated on page 26

HARICOT BEANS WITH APPLE AND CIDER

INGREDIENTS

8oz (250g) haricot beans, soaked
2 tsp (10ml) sunflower oil
1 onion, chopped
2 medium carrots, finely sliced
8oz (250g) sweet potato, diced
2 tsp (10ml) fresh basil
2 tsp (10ml) fresh marjoram
1/2 pint (300ml) dry cider
2 eating apples, diced
4oz (125g) pineapple flesh, diced
4oz (125g) black grapes, halved

•

NUTRITION PROFILE

*This dish contains calcium, iron, copper,
zinc, Vitamins A, B_1, B_6, C and E.*

• Per portion •
Carbohydrate: 62g
Protein: 15.1g **Fibre:** 20.4g
Fat: 3.9g **Calories:** 340

*This casserole is good hot or cold, served with a fresh green salad and a
garnish of marjoram. The cider enhances the fruity flavour, while the
herbs offset the beans and vegetables.*

Preparation time: 40 mins (plus 10–12 hours soaking time)
Cooking time: 2–3 mins (plus 50 mins for the beans)
Serves 4

METHOD

1. Drain the beans. Put into a saucepan with fresh water. Bring to
the boil and boil fast for 10 minutes. Reduce the heat, cover and
simmer for 40 minutes or until tender. Drain well.

2. Heat the oil in a large pan and fry the onion for 5 minutes. Add
the carrots, sweet potato, beans, basil and marjoram and cook for
5 minutes. Add the cider, cover and simmer for 10 minutes.

3. Add the apples, pineapple and deseeded grapes. Continue
cooking for 2–3 minutes. Serve hot or cold.

Illustrated on page 26

GIANT WHOLEMEAL SAMOSA

INGREDIENTS

FILLING
6oz (175g) mung beans, soaked
2 medium potatoes, diced
2 tsp (10ml) sunflower oil
1 large onion, chopped
1 tsp (5ml) cumin seeds
2 cloves garlic, chopped
1 tbsp (15ml) mild curry powder
¼ pint (150ml) mung bean stock
or water
1 tbsp (15ml) shoyu

PASTRY
8oz (250g) fine wholemeal flour
2oz (50g) butter or vegetable margarine
2oz (50g) white vegetable fat
pinch chilli powder
5–6 tbsp (75–90ml) cold water

•

NUTRITION PROFILE

This is rich in iron, copper, zinc, folic acid, niacin and Vitamins A, B_1, B_6, C, D and E.

• Per portion •
Carbohydrate: 70.3g
Protein: 20.5g **Fibre:** 17.1g
Fat: 28.4g **Calories:** 605

Light wholemeal pastry is here filled with the traditional spicy mixture of mung beans and potatoes and garnished with parsley.

Preparation time: 45 mins (plus 10–12 hours soaking time for the beans, and 15–30 mins resting time for the pastry dough)
Cooking time: 30 mins (plus 30 mins for the beans)
Serves 4–6

METHOD

1. Drain the beans. Boil fast in fresh water for 10 minutes. Then cover and simmer for 20 minutes. Drain and reserve the stock.

2. Meanwhile, put the potatoes in a pan, cover with water, simmer until just tender, then drain and leave to cool slightly.

3. Heat the oil in a pan and fry the onion, cumin seeds and garlic for 5 minutes. Sprinkle over the curry powder and add the mung beans and potatoes. Cook for 2–3 minutes. Pour on the mung bean stock and shoyu. Cook gently for 5 minutes, then cool.

4. Make the pastry (see below), if necessary adding extra water to make the dough moist. Cover and leave to rest for 15–30 minutes. Roll out the pastry to a 12 inch (30cm) square. Put the cooled mung bean mixture on to the pastry and seal (see below).

5. Place on a baking tray, glaze with milk. Bake in a preheated oven at Gas Mark 6, 400°F, 200°C for 30 minutes. Serve hot or cold.

Illustrated on page 26

MAKING SAMOSAS

A samosa is a savoury snack from Asia, in which a spicy filling is wrapped up in pastry to make a triangular parcel and then traditionally deep-fried, although here it is baked. Pastry is not known for its nutritional value, but using wholemeal instead of white flour makes a pastry which contains useful amounts of fibre, protein, vitamins and minerals. It is important to make the dough fairly moist and then allow it to rest.

1. Combine the flour and fat. Add the chilli. Sprinkle on 3–4 tbsp (45–60ml) water, form into a dough, leave to rest.

2. Roll out the pastry to a 12 inch (30cm) square. Place the filling in a diamond shape on the pastry.

3. Draw up the two front corners of the pastry, dampen the edges and seal. Repeat for the two back corners.

BLACK BEANS AND OLIVES

INGREDIENTS

8oz (250g) black beans, soaked
2oz (50g) small wholemeal pasta shells
2 tsp (10ml) olive oil
2 onions, chopped
2 cloves garlic, crushed
4oz (125g) button mushrooms
1 tbsp (15ml) chopped fresh rosemary
12 black olives, stoned and sliced
1 tbsp (15ml) chopped capers
2 tbsp (30ml) lemon juice
1 tbsp (15ml) cider vinegar
1 tbsp (15ml) tomato purée

•

NUTRITION PROFILE

This meal is rich in copper, zinc, iron, folic acid, niacin, Vitamins B$_1$, C and E.

• Per portion •
Carbohydrate: 41.4g
Protein: 17.2g   **Fibre:** 17.5g
Fat: 5.3g   **Calories:** 280

Black beans and black olives make a delicious combination. Garnish with rosemary and lemon.

Preparation time: 25 mins (plus 10–12 hours soaking time)
Cooking time: 10 mins (plus 40 mins for the beans)
Serves 4

METHOD

1. Drain the black beans. Cover with fresh water, bring to the boil and boil fast for 10 minutes. Reduce the heat, cover and simmer for 30 minutes, then drain.

2. Cook the pasta shells in boiling water for 5 minutes. Drain.

3. Heat the oil in a large pan and fry the onion and garlic for 5 minutes. Add the beans, mushrooms and rosemary, cover and cook for 5 minutes. Stir in the pasta shells, olives, capers, lemon juice and cider vinegar. Dissolve the tomato purée in $1/4$ pint (150ml) of water and pour over the beans. Cover and cook gently for 10 minutes. Serve hot or cold.

Illustrated opposite

CURRIED CHICK PEAS

INGREDIENTS

6oz (175g) chick peas, soaked
2 tsp (10ml) sunflower oil
2 onions, chopped
2 cloves garlic, crushed
1 tsp (5ml) cumin seeds
8oz (250g) potatoes, cut into pieces
1 tsp (5ml) ground cumin
1 tsp (5ml) ground coriander
1 tsp (5ml) turmeric
$1/4$ tsp chilli powder
1oz (25g) raisins
1oz (25g) blanched almonds, chopped

•

NUTRITION PROFILE

This dish provides iron, copper, calcium, folic acid, Vitamins B$_1$, C and E.

• Per portion •
Carbohydrate: 44.1g
Protein: 12.7g   **Fibre:** 9.9g
Fat: 9.4g   **Calories:** 305

Traditionally known as Channa Dhal. Serve with brown rice and a natural yogurt, cucumber and mint salad. Garnish with coriander.

Preparation time: 15 mins (plus 10–12 hours soaking time)
Cooking time: 35 mins (plus 50 mins for the chick peas)
Serves 4

METHOD

1. Drain the chick peas. Cover with fresh water, bring to the boil and boil fast for 10 minutes. Reduce the heat, cover and simmer for 40 minutes. Drain and reserve the stock.

2. Heat the oil in a pan and fry the onion, garlic and cumin seeds for 5 minutes. Add the potatoes, chick peas and spices and cook for 3–4 minutes.

3. Pour over $3/4$ pint (450ml) reserved stock. Cover and simmer for 25–30 minutes. Add the raisins, cook for a further 3–4 minutes, stir in the almonds, check the seasoning and serve hot.

Illustrated on page 29

Clockwise from top: **Giant wholemeal samosa** (*see p.25*); **Black beans and olives** (*see above*); **Butter beans au gratin** (*see p.24*); **Haricot beans with apple and cider** (*see p.24*).

QUICK RED LENTILS

INGREDIENTS

8oz (250g) red split lentils
1 onion, finely chopped
1 clove garlic, crushed
2 sticks celery, finely chopped
1 tsp (5ml) ground cumin
1 tsp (5ml) garam masala
¼ tsp chilli powder
1 tsp (5ml) turmeric
1 bay leaf
1 pint (600ml) water
2 tsp (10ml) lemon juice
1 tbsp (15ml) shoyu
½oz (15g) creamed coconut,
finely chopped

TOPPING
2 tsp (10ml) sunflower oil
1 onion, sliced into fine rings

•

NUTRITION PROFILE

*This recipe is high in protein. It is also a good
source of fibre and of iron, zinc, copper,
magnesium, Vitamins B_1 and B_6.*

• Per portion •
Carbohydrate: 39.1g
Protein: 16.1g   **Fibre:** 9.4g
Fat: 6.9g   **Calories:** 275

*Red lentils are ideal for a quick, healthy meal, and are a good base for
any distinctive flavour. Here they are subtly spiced, then topped with
crisp-fried onion rings. Serve with brown rice or steamed broccoli, and
garnish with lemon wedges. If you want to reduce the fat content, leave
out the fried onion rings. If you are using lentils that are not ready-
prepared, remember to pick over for stones.*

Preparation time: 10 mins   Cooking time: 25 mins
Serves 4

METHOD

1. Wash the lentils. Put them into a large pan with the onion,
garlic, celery, cumin, garam masala, chilli powder, turmeric,
bay leaf and fresh water. Bring to the boil, cover the pan and
simmer gently for 20–25 minutes until the liquid has
been absorbed.

2. Remove the bay leaf, beat the lentil mixture into a smooth
paste with a wooden spoon. Add the lemon juice, shoyu and
creamed coconut. Check the seasoning.

3. For the topping, heat the oil in a frying pan and quickly fry the
onion rings until browned, taking care that they do not burn.

4. Serve the lentils hot, topped with the crisp onion rings.

Illustrated opposite

Clockwise from top: **Quick red lentils** (*see above*); **Curried chick peas** (*see p. 27*); **Haricot beans and tomato sauce** (*see p. 30*).

HARICOT BEANS AND TOMATO SAUCE

INGREDIENTS

8oz (250g) haricot beans, soaked
2 tsp (10ml) sunflower oil
1 large onion, chopped
1 clove garlic, crushed
2 medium carrots, grated
1 dessert apple, cored and grated
14oz (400g) can of chopped tomatoes
2 tbsp (30ml) tomato purée
1 tsp (5ml) paprika
pinch chilli powder
1 bay leaf
1 tbsp (15ml) shoyu
1 tsp (5ml) concentrated apple juice
3 fl oz (75ml) water

•

NUTRITION PROFILE

*These beans contain zinc, copper, niacin
and Vitamins A, B_1, B_6, C and E.*

• Per portion •
Carbohydrate: 39.9g
Protein: 15.9g **Fibre:** 18.8g
Fat: 3.7g **Calories:** 245

*This fruity, saltless recipe has a rich tomato sauce to offset the
creaminess of the beans. Serve with a green salad.*

Preparation time: 20 mins (plus 10–12 hours soaking time)
Cooking time: 40 mins (plus 50 mins for the beans)
Serves 4

METHOD

1. Drain the beans. Cover with fresh water, bring to the boil and
boil fast for 10 minutes. Reduce the heat, cover and simmer for 40
minutes. Drain and set aside.

2. Heat the oil in a pan and gently fry the onion and garlic for
about 5 minutes. Add the beans and cook for 2–3 minutes.

3. Add the carrots, apple, tomatoes, tomato purée, paprika, chilli
powder, bay leaf, shoyu and concentrated apple juice or honey.

4. Bring to the boil, cover and simmer gently for 30–40 minutes,
adding a little water if the mixture seems dry. Remove the bay
leaf, check the seasoning and serve hot.

Illustrated on page 29

CRUNCHY CASSEROLE WITH CHICK PEAS

INGREDIENTS

4oz (125g) chick peas, soaked
2 medium carrots cut into strips
1 small head fennel, sliced thinly
1 tsp (5ml) caraway seeds
2 oz (50g) French beans, trimmed
1 small red pepper, sliced thinly
¼ pint (150ml) water
3 tbsp (45ml) natural yogurt
1 tbsp (15ml) mayonnaise
1 clove garlic, crushed

•

NUTRITION PROFILE

*This dish is rich in Vitamins A, C, folic
acid, iron, magnesium and calcium.*

• Per portion •
Carbohydrate: 21.3g
Protein: 9g **Fibre:** 10.6g
Fat: 5.2g **Calories:** 160

This is a very healthy and filling hot or cold accompaniment to a main dish.

Preparation time: 10 mins (plus 10–12 hours soaking time)
Cooking time: 15 mins (plus 50 mins for the beans)
Serves 4

METHOD

1. Drain the chick peas and boil fast in fresh water for 10 minutes.
Simmer for 40 minutes. Drain well.

2. Put the chick peas into a casserole. Cover with thin strips of
carrots and fennel. Sprinkle with caraway seeds. Layer the French
beans and red pepper strips on top. Sprinkle on 2 tbsp (30ml)
fresh parsley. Pour over the stock or water. Cover and bake in a
preheated oven at Gas Mark 4, 350°F, 180°C for 15 minutes.
Pour on the dressing of yogurt, mayonnaise and garlic mixed
together and serve hot or cold.

Illustrated opposite

Top: **Crunchy casserole with chick peas** (*see above*); Bottom: **Aubergine and butter bean biryani** (*see p.32*).

AUBERGINE ~ BUTTER BEAN BIRYANI

INGREDIENTS

3oz (75g) butter beans, soaked
2 tsp (10ml) sunflower oil
1 tsp (5ml) poppy seeds
1 tsp (5ml) mustard seeds
8oz (250g) long-grain brown rice
1/4 tsp chilli powder
1 tsp (5ml) turmeric
1 tsp (5ml) garam masala
1 tsp (5ml) ground coriander
2 tbsp (30ml) cold water
1 medium aubergine, diced
1 large red pepper, deseeded and cut
into strips
14oz (400g) can of tomatoes
cold water or butter bean stock
1 tbsp (15ml) shoyu
1/2oz (15g) creamed coconut, grated
(or 3 tbsp/45ml natural yogurt)

•

NUTRITION PROFILE

*A high-fibre, high-protein meal that is also
rich in magnesium, copper, zinc, iron, folic
acid, niacin and Vitamins B₁, C and E.*

• Per portion •
Carbohydrate: 67.7g
Protein: 12.2g **Fibre:** 10.4g
Fat: 8.8g **Calories:** 375

*A biryani is an Indian-style paella. Here, butter beans and aubergines
are combined with mildly spiced rice to make a delicious, well-balanced
meal. If you prefer to use canned butter beans, double the quantity,
and, to prevent them becoming too soft, add to the biryani 10 minutes
from the end of the cooking time. If you want to reduce the fat content,
use natural yogurt instead of creamed coconut.*

Preparation time: 25 mins (plus 10–12 hours soaking time)
Cooking time: 30–40 mins (plus 1 hour for the beans)
Serves 4

METHOD

1. Drain the beans. Put in a saucepan and cover with fresh water.
Bring to the boil and boil fast for 10 minutes. Reduce the heat,
cover and simmer for 50 minutes or until just tender. Drain well,
reserving the stock.

2. Heat the oil in a large pan. Gently cook the poppy and mustard
seeds until they begin to pop. Add the rice and continue cooking
gently for 3–4 minutes.

3. In a separate bowl mix together the chilli powder, turmeric,
garam masala and coriander, adding 2 tbsp (30ml) cold water to
make a paste. Pour the paste over the rice, then add the
aubergine, red pepper and butter beans, coating them well. Cook
gently for 3–4 minutes.

4. Drain the tomatoes, reserving the juice, and add them to the
rice mixture. Make the juice up to 1 pint (600ml) with the water
or bean stock and pour on to the rice. Add the shoyu.

5. Cover and simmer for 30–40 minutes until the rice is cooked
and most of the liquid is absorbed. Stir in the creamed coconut or
yogurt. Check the seasoning and serve hot.

Illustrated on page 31

VEGETABLES

Vegetables, enriched with flavours from around the world, make a nutritious and versatile base in a wide range of dishes. Combine with pulses, grains, pastry and dairy products for filling main courses, or with nuts, seeds and fruit for appetizing side dishes. Stuffed vegetables make attractive centrepieces and can be main or side dishes.

SAVOURY CRUMBLE

INGREDIENTS

2 tsp (10ml) sunflower oil
1 onion, chopped
4oz (125g) mushrooms, sliced if large
4oz (125g) carrots, sliced
1 small cauliflower, cut into florets
2 tsp (10ml) chopped fresh rosemary
1 tbsp (15ml) wholemeal flour
$\frac{1}{2}$ pint (300ml) water
1 tsp (5ml) miso or yeast extract
2 tbsp (30ml) boiling water
$\frac{1}{4}$ tsp black pepper

TOPPING
3oz (75g) jumbo or porridge oats
1oz (25g) blanched almonds, chopped
1 tbsp (15ml) sunflower oil

•

NUTRITION PROFILE

This high-fibre dish is rich in Vitamins A, B₁, C and E, niacin, folic acid, iron and magnesium.

• Per portion •
Carbohydrate: 21.9g
Protein: 7.8g   **Fibre:** 9.2g
Fat: 11.7g   **Calories:** 220

This mixed vegetable casserole is made more unusual and more nutritious by a nutty crumble topping. Various combinations of vegetables can be used according to season and choice. Jumbo oats in the topping give a very crunchy texture, but the smaller porridge oats can be used instead. Serve with a garnish of rosemary.

Preparation time: 40 mins   Cooking time: 30 mins
Serves 4

METHOD

1. Heat the oil over a moderate heat in a large frying pan and fry the onion, mushrooms, carrots and cauliflower. Cover and cook for 10 minutes, stirring frequently.

2. Sprinkle on the rosemary and flour and cook for 2–3 minutes. Pour on the water, bring to the boil and simmer gently for 5 minutes. Stir in the miso or yeast extract (dissolved in the boiling water) and the pepper. Put the mixture into a casserole or ovenproof dish.

3. For the topping, mix together the oats, almonds and oil. Sprinkle on top of the vegetables.

4. Bake in a preheated oven at Gas Mark 4, 350°F, 180°C for 30 minutes. Serve hot.

Illustrated on page 34

VEGETABLE AND LENTIL COTTAGE PIE

INGREDIENTS
8oz (250g) brown lentils
2 bay leaves
2 tsp (10ml) sunflower oil
1 onion, finely chopped
4oz (125g) carrots, finely chopped
3 sticks celery, diced
2 tsp (10ml) paprika
1 tsp (5ml) chopped fresh marjoram
1 tsp (5ml) chopped fresh sage
1 tbsp (15ml) tomato purée
1 tbsp (15ml) shoyu
1 tsp (5ml) yeast extract
½ pint (300ml) lentil stock or water
1 lb (500g) potatoes, chopped
½oz (15g) vegetable margarine
2 tbsp (30ml) skimmed milk
2 large tomatoes, sliced
2 tsp (10ml) sesame seeds

GARNISH
sprig of sage
sprig of marjoram

•
NUTRITION PROFILE
*This low-fat, high-protein, high-fibre dish
is rich in iron, zinc, copper, magnesium,
folic acid, niacin and Vitamins A, B_1, B_2,
B_6, C and E.*

• Per portion •
Carbohydrate: 64.9g
Protein: 20.3g **Fibre:** 11.8g
Fat: 8g **Calories:** 400

*German or brown lentils are used here to create a simple yet substantial
family meal. If you are using lentils that are not ready-prepared,
remember to rinse them well and pick over for stones. Try serving with
lightly steamed green vegetables and a tomato sauce, and garnish with
sage and marjoram.*

Preparation time: 1 hour   Cooking time: 30 mins
Serves 4

METHOD

1. Wash the lentils. Cover with plenty of cold water in a large
saucepan. Add the bay leaves, bring to the boil, cover the pan
and simmer gently for 25 minutes or until the lentils are soft.
Drain well and reserve the stock. Remove the bay leaves and
set aside.

2. Heat the oil in a large saucepan and fry the onion, carrots and
celery for 5 minutes.

3. Add the cooked lentils, the paprika, marjoram and sage
together with the tomato purée, shoyu, yeast extract and lentil
stock. Cover and simmer gently for 15–20 minutes. Check
the seasoning.

4. Meanwhile, boil the potatoes until cooked. Drain, add
the margarine and milk, and mash well.

5. Put the lentil mixture into the base of a large casserole. Cover
with sliced tomatoes. Top with the mashed potato. Sprinkle over
the sesame seeds, and bake in a preheated oven at Gas Mark 4,
350°F, 180°C for 30 minutes. Add the garnish of herbs and
serve hot.

Illustrated opposite

Clockwise from top: **Savoury crumble** (*see p.33*); **Baked tomatoes** (*see p.36*); **Vegetable and lentil cottage pie** (*see above*).

BAKED TOMATOES

INGREDIENTS

8 large tomatoes
2 tsp (10ml) olive oil
1 onion, finely chopped
4oz (125g) mushrooms, finely chopped
2oz (50g) blanched almonds, chopped
2 tsp (10ml) chopped fresh thyme
pinch chilli powder
4oz (125g) wholemeal breadcrumbs
2 tsp (10ml) shoyu
½ tsp black pepper
3 fl oz (75ml) water

•

NUTRITION PROFILE

This dish is a good source of Vitamins C and E, iron, fibre and folic acid.

• Per portion •
Carbohydrate: 16.4g
Protein: 6.4g **Fibre:** 6.7g
Fat: 10.3g **Calories:** 180

Served hot or cold, these savoury tomatoes make a simple, appetizing meal. Choose firm tomatoes, since these will not collapse in the heat of the oven. Garnish with lemon and thyme.

Preparation time: 30 mins   Cooking time: 25 mins
Serves 4 (as a main course)

METHOD

1. Slice the tops off the tomatoes, scoop out and reserve the flesh and seeds. Put the tomato cases into an ovenproof dish.

2. Heat the oil and fry the onion for 4–5 minutes. Add the mushrooms, almonds, thyme and chilli powder. Cover and cook gently for another 7–10 minutes. Add the breadcrumbs, tomato flesh and seeds, shoyu and pepper. Check the seasoning.

3. Stuff the tomato cases and replace the tops. Pour the water into the dish. Bake in a preheated oven at Gas Mark 5, 375°F, 190°C for 25 minutes.

Illustrated on page 34

CHEESY LEEK ᴬᴺᴰ POTATO CASSEROLE

INGREDIENTS

1 lb (500g) leeks, cut into ¾ inch (1.5cm) slices
1 lb (500g) potatoes, cut into ¼ inch (5mm) slices
1½oz (40g) vegetable margarine
1oz (25g) wholemeal flour
½ pint (300ml) skimmed milk
½ tsp mustard powder or Dijon mustard
¼ tsp black pepper
2oz (50g) Cheddar cheese, grated

•

NUTRITION PROFILE

This high-fibre, high-protein dish is a good source of Vitamins A, B_6, B_{12}, C, D and E, calcium and iron.

• Per portion •
Carbohydrate: 41.4g
Protein: 11.7g **Fibre:** 7g
Fat: 12.8g **Calories:** 315

Steam the leeks carefully so that they remain slightly crunchy. Use a mature cheese for maximum flavour and minimum calories.

Preparation time: 40 mins   Cooking time: 25 mins
Serves 4

METHOD

1. Steam the leeks over a large pan of simmering water for 8 minutes.

2. Meanwhile, cover the potato slices with water. Bring to the boil and simmer gently for 10 minutes. Drain well.

3. Melt the margarine, add the flour and cook gently, stirring, for 2–3 minutes. Remove from the heat, gradually stir in the milk. Return to the heat and bring to the boil, stirring constantly. Cook gently for 2–3 minutes. Stir in the mustard and pepper.

4. Layer the leeks and potato in a casserole or ovenproof dish. Pour the sauce over the top and sprinkle with grated cheese. Bake in a preheated oven at Gas Mark 4, 350°F, 180°C for 25 minutes until golden brown. Serve hot.

Illustrated opposite

Clockwise from top: **Ratatouille** (*see p. 38*); **Vegetable curry** (*see p. 39*); **Cheesy leek and potato casserole** (*see above*).

RATATOUILLE

INGREDIENTS

2 tsp (10ml) olive oil
1 medium onion, chopped
2 cloves garlic, chopped
1 small aubergine, chopped
1 red pepper, deseeded and thinly sliced
2 medium courgettes, sliced
14oz (400g) can of chopped tomatoes
$\frac{1}{2}$ tsp chopped fresh basil
$\frac{1}{2}$ tsp chopped fresh thyme
$\frac{1}{2}$ tsp chopped fresh oregano
1 bay leaf
2 tbsp (30ml) tomato purée
$\frac{1}{2}$ tsp black pepper

•

NUTRITION PROFILE

*This low-calorie dish is rich in Vitamins A,
C and E, and in folic acid and iron.*

• Per portion •
Carbohydrate: 9.2g
Protein: 3.2g **Fibre:** 3.4g
Fat: 2.8g **Calories:** 70

*Ratatouille is a traditional vegetable stew from Provence, usually made
with plenty of olive oil. This is a much healthier version, and well
flavoured with a mixture of Mediterranean herbs.*

Preparation time: 15 mins   Cooking time: 50 mins
Serves 4

METHOD

1. Heat the oil in a saucepan and fry the onion and garlic for
5 minutes.

2. Add the rest of the ingredients, cover and simmer very gently
for 50 minutes, stirring occasionally. Add a little water if the
mixture seems dry.

3. Remove the bay leaf, check the seasoning and serve hot
or cold.

Illustrated on page 37

STUFFED AUBERGINES WITH APRICOTS

INGREDIENTS

2 small aubergines
8oz (250g) red split lentils
2 tsp (10ml) olive oil
1 small onion, finely chopped
$\frac{1}{2}$ tsp ground cumin
$\frac{1}{2}$ tsp ground coriander
3oz (75g) dried apricots, chopped
1 tbsp (15ml) concentrated apple juice
3 tbsp (45ml) lentil stock or water

•

NUTRITION PROFILE

*High in protein and fibre but low in fat,
this dish is also rich in copper, zinc, iron,
magnesium, folic acid and Vitamins
B_6 and C.*

• Per portion •
Carbohydrate: 47.2g
Protein: 16.9g **Fibre:** 14.7g
Fat: 3.4g **Calories:** 275

*Serve this healthy version of a traditional Turkish dish with a tomato
sauce and a crisp green pepper and lettuce salad.*

Preparation time: 45 mins   Cooking time: 45 mins
Serves 4

METHOD

1. Cut the aubergines in half and scoop out (see opposite).

2. Cover the lentils with water. Bring to the boil, cover and
simmer for 15–20 minutes. Drain, and reserve any excess liquid.

3. Heat the oil over a moderate heat and gently cook the onion,
cumin and coriander for 5 minutes. Stir in the aubergine flesh and
drained lentils and cook for 5–8 minutes. Add the apricots,
concentrated apple juice, 1 tbsp (15ml) shoyu and the stock or
water. Cook for a further 5 minutes. Check the seasoning.

4. Fill the aubergine shells with the mixture. Cover and bake in a
preheated oven at Gas Mark 5, 375°F, 190°C for 45 minutes.

Illustrated on page 40

STUFFING AN AUBERGINE

Scooped-out vegetables and fruits make a convenient and attractive way of serving a dish. Aubergine plays an essential part in Mediterranean food, although it actually originates from Asia. Stuffed aubergine is a traditional dish in Greece and Turkey, where it is often served with minced meat; apricots and lentils are another authentic filling. The beautiful rich colour of the skin makes this dish look most appetizing.

1. Slash the aubergine flesh, taking care not to damage the skin. Scoop out and chop finely.

2. Heat the oil and spices in a pan. Add the other ingredients and cook as directed in the recipe.

3. Spoon the mixture back into the aubergine halves. Cover and bake.

VEGETABLE CURRY

INGREDIENTS

2 tsp (10ml) sunflower oil
1 tsp (5ml) cumin seeds
1 tsp (5ml) coriander seeds
1 large onion, finely chopped
3 cloves garlic, crushed
1 tsp (5ml) garam masala
¼ tsp chilli powder
1 medium potato, finely diced
1 parsnip, cut into small chunks
1 courgette, sliced
1 green pepper, deseeded and cut into strips
1 small aubergine, diced
2 tbsp (30ml) wholemeal flour
14oz (400g) can of chopped tomatoes
¼ pint (150ml) water or stock
1oz (25g) creamed coconut, grated
1 tbsp (15ml) shoyu

•

NUTRITION PROFILE

This recipe is high in Vitamins A, C and E, and in folic acid and iron.

• Per portion •
Carbohydrate: 19.6g
Protein: 7.1g   **Fibre:** 7.2g
Fat: 8.9g   **Calories:** 180

This mixed vegetable curry is good served with plain brown rice and poppadums. If made a day in advance, the flavours of the curry have more time to develop. If you do not have the various spices, use 1–2 tbsp (15–30ml) mild curry powder.

Preparation time: 30 mins   Cooking time: 40 mins
Serves 4

METHOD

1. Heat the oil over a moderate heat in a large pan. Gently cook the cumin and coriander seeds for 4–5 minutes until the seeds are turning brown. Add the onion, garlic, garam masala and chilli powder, and continue cooking gently for a further 5 minutes.

2. Add the potato, parsnip, courgette, green pepper and aubergine to the pan. Continue cooking for 5 minutes, stirring well to ensure that the vegetables are well coated in spices. Sprinkle over the flour and cook for 2–3 minutes.

3. Add the tomatoes and their juice, together with the water or stock. Cover and simmer for 40 minutes, stirring occasionally and adding a little extra water or stock if necessary.

4. When the vegetables are tender, add the creamed coconut and shoyu. Check the seasoning and serve hot.

Illustrated on page 37

BAKED SPANISH OMELETTE

INGREDIENTS

10oz (300g) potatoes, diced
4oz (125g) carrots, diced
4oz (125g) sweetcorn, fresh, frozen
or canned
$\frac{1}{2}$ tsp sunflower oil
1 small courgette, thinly sliced
1 small red pepper, cut into thin strips
12 black olives, stoned
4 eggs, well beaten
7 fl oz (200ml) skimmed milk
1 tsp (5ml) chopped fresh thyme
$\frac{1}{2}$ tsp paprika
1 clove garlic, crushed
2 large tomatoes, thinly sliced
1$\frac{1}{2}$oz (40g) Cheddar cheese, grated
•

NUTRITION PROFILE

*This omelette contains Vitamins A, B$_2$,
B$_{12}$, C, D and E, iron, calcium and zinc.*

• Per portion •
Carbohydrate: 27.9g
Protein: 14.2g **Fibre:** 5.6g
Fat: 11g **Calories:** 260

*This recipe is like a quiche without the pastry case, which keeps the fat
and calorie content down. Vary the vegetables according to season.*

Preparation time: 30 mins   Cooking time: 45 mins
Serves 4

METHOD

1. Cover the potatoes and carrots with plenty of water, bring to
the boil and simmer gently for 10 minutes. If using fresh
sweetcorn, add to the potatoes and carrots for the last 4–5
minutes. Drain and set aside.

2. Lightly oil an 8 inch (20cm) round dish. Put in the potatoes,
carrots and sweetcorn. Cover with slices of courgette and pepper,
and the olives.

3. Mix together the eggs, milk, thyme, paprika and garlic. Season
and then pour over the vegetable mixture. Cover with slices of
tomato and grated cheese.

4. Bake in a preheated oven at Gas Mark 5, 375°F, 190°C for 45
minutes or until golden brown and set. Serve hot.

Illustrated opposite

CHINESE BAKE WITH WATERCRESS SAUCE

INGREDIENTS

1$\frac{1}{2}$lb (750g) Chinese cabbage
8oz (250g) cottage cheese with chives
$\frac{1}{4}$ tsp black pepper
1oz (25g) vegetable margarine
1 bunch watercress, chopped
1 small onion, chopped
1 clove garlic, chopped
2 tbsp (30ml) grated Parmesan cheese
•

NUTRITION PROFILE

*This bake is rich in iron, calcium,
magnesium, copper, folic acid and
Vitamins A, B$_{12}$, C and D.*

• Per portion •
Carbohydrate: 9.6g
Protein: 17.6g **Fibre:** 6.2g
Fat: 8.9g **Calories:** 180

Serve with potatoes and a carrot salad for a balanced, low-calorie meal.

Preparation time: 35 mins   Cooking time: 25 mins
Serves 4

METHOD

1. Cut the leafy part from the cabbage, and steam the stems gently
for 3–4 minutes. Put the cottage cheese into a large casserole dish,
sprinkle with black pepper and cover with the stems.

2. Melt the margarine slowly. Add the chopped cabbage leaves,
watercress, onion and garlic. Cover and cook gently for 7–8
minutes. Cool slightly, then purée until smooth.

3. Pour the watercress mixture over the cottage cheese and stems.
Sprinkle over the Parmesan cheese and bake in a preheated oven
at Gas Mark 4, 350°F, 180°C for 25 minutes. Serve hot.

Illustrated opposite

Clockwise from top: **Baked Spanish omelette** (*see above*); **Stuffed aubergines with apricots** (*see p. 38*);
Chinese bake with watercress sauce (*see above*).

MEXICAN PIZZA

INGREDIENTS

BASE
4oz (125g) cornmeal
4oz (125g) wholemeal flour
1½ tsp (7.5ml) baking powder
¼ tsp mustard powder
¼ tsp salt
1 egg, beaten
8 fl oz (250ml) skimmed milk

TOPPING
2 tsp (10ml) olive oil
1 onion, chopped
1 clove garlic, crushed
8oz (250g) courgettes, sliced
14oz (400g) can of chopped tomatoes
2 tbsp (30ml) tomato purée
2 tsp (10ml) chopped fresh oregano
12 black olives, stoned
3oz (75g) Cheddar cheese, grated

•

NUTRITION PROFILE

This pizza is high in fibre and protein and rich in Vitamins A, B_1, B_2, B_{12}, C and E, niacin, calcium, iron, zinc, magnesium and folic acid.

• Per portion •
Carbohydrate: 54.8g
Protein: 18.5g   **Fibre:** 9.4g
Fat: 13.2g   **Calories:** 405

This is a pizza-style dish with a base made from cornmeal, a bright yellow flour traditionally used to make Mexican tortillas and cornbreads. It is made from a 95 per cent extraction of maize and is therefore high in nutrients and fibre. When courgettes are unavailable, try using mushrooms instead.

Preparation time: 50 mins   Cooking time: 20 mins
Serves 4

METHOD

1. For the base, mix together the cornmeal, wholemeal flour, baking powder, mustard powder and salt in a large bowl.

2. In a separate bowl, beat together the egg and milk.

3. Pour the egg and milk into the flour and, using a spoon, draw it together into a soft dough. Spread out the dough in a lightly oiled 9 inch (23cm) round flan ring or 8 inch (20cm) square tin.

4. Bake in a preheated oven at Gas Mark 6, 400°F, 200°C for 10 minutes, then set aside. Reduce the oven temperature to Gas Mark 5, 375°F, 190°C.

5. For the topping, heat the oil over a moderate heat in a large pan and gently fry the onion and garlic for 5 minutes.

6. Add the courgettes and continue frying for a further 5 minutes.

7. Add the tomatoes, tomato purée and oregano, cover and simmer for 15 minutes to form a thick sauce adding a little water or tomato juice if needed.

8. Stir in the olives, then spread the sauce on top of the base. Cover with the grated cheese.

9. Bake in the oven for 20 minutes. Serve immediately.

Illustrated opposite

Clockwise from top right: **English vegetable casserole** (see p.44); **Tomatoes and basil with a crisp potato topping** (see p.44); **Mexican pizza** (see above).

ENGLISH VEGETABLE CASSEROLE

INGREDIENTS

2 tsp (10ml) sunflower oil
1 onion, finely chopped
2 tbsp (30ml) wholemeal flour
14oz (400g) can of chopped tomatoes
1 tbsp (15ml) shoyu
1 tsp (5ml) chopped fresh sage
1 tsp (5ml) chopped fresh thyme
3 tbsp (45ml) chopped fresh parsley
$\frac{1}{2}$ tsp black pepper
8oz (250g) leeks, sliced
4oz (125g) shallots, peeled
4oz (125g) carrots, thinly sliced
4oz (125g) mushrooms, sliced if large
4oz (125g) parsnips, thinly sliced
4oz (125g) celery, chopped
1 medium potato, thinly sliced

•

NUTRITION PROFILE

*This is rich in Vitamins A, B_1, B_6, C, E,
folic acid, iron, calcium and copper.*

• Per portion •
Carbohydrate: 26.4g
Protein: 6.1g   **Fibre:** 9g
Fat: 3.4g   **Calories:** 155

*This dish can be served as a simple lunch or supper dish with crusty
French bread, but also makes an excellent accompaniment to lentil
burgers or a nut loaf.*

Preparation time: 30 mins   Cooking time: 45 mins
Serves 4

METHOD

1. Heat the oil in a large pan over a moderate heat and gently fry
the onion for 4–5 minutes. Sprinkle over the flour and cook for
2–3 minutes. Add the tomatoes and their juice together with the
shoyu, sage, thyme, parsley and black pepper. Cook gently for
3–5 minutes.

2. Add the rest of the vegetables, except the potato, to the pan
and simmer gently for 5 minutes, adding a little water if the
mixture seems dry.

3. Put the vegetable mixture into a large casserole or ovenproof
dish. Top with the sliced potato and brush with a little extra oil.
Cover the casserole and bake in a preheated oven at Gas Mark 4,
350°F, 180°C for 45 minutes. Remove the lid for the last
10 minutes.

Illustrated on page 43

TOMATOES ^{AND} BASIL
WITH A CRISP POTATO TOPPING

INGREDIENTS

1 lb (500g) potatoes, sliced
$\frac{1}{2}$oz (15g) vegetable margarine
2–3 tbsp (30–45ml) skimmed milk
$\frac{1}{4}$ tsp black pepper
14oz (400g) can of tomatoes, drained
2 tsp (10ml) chopped fresh basil
2oz (50g) Cheddar cheese, grated

•

NUTRITION PROFILE

*This recipe is a good source of calcium and
Vitamins A, B_6, B_{12}, C and D.*

• Per portion •
Carbohydrate: 28.5g
Protein: 7.3g   **Fibre:** 3.5g
Fat: 7.4g   **Calories:** 200

*Serve these creamy potatoes with a root-, shoot- or fruit-based salad. If
you like a decorative finish, try piping the potato on the top.*

Preparation time: 30 mins   Cooking time: 25 mins
Serves 4

METHOD

1. Cover the potatoes with plenty of cold water. Bring to the boil,
cover and simmer for 15–20 minutes or until soft. Drain, add the
margarine, milk and black pepper and mash.

2. Place the tomatoes in an ovenproof dish. Sprinkle with basil,
top with mashed potato, then sprinkle with the grated cheese.

3. Bake in a preheated oven at Gas Mark 5, 375°F, 190°C for 25
minutes until golden brown.

Illustrated on page 43

MAKING POTATO TOPPINGS

Potatoes are one of the most versatile vegetables. Certain cooking methods like baking in jackets or boiling in skins are the most nutritious ways of preparing them. Mashed potato makes an attractive and tasty topping. The mixture should be smooth and moist, but peel the potatoes only if you want to pipe them.

1. Use 2 dessertspoons of mashed potato to make oval potato cakes. Place on top of the dish.

2. Use a star-shaped nozzle and piping bag to pipe small spirals of potato in rows across the dish.

3. Place a layer of potato over the vegetables, and decorate with the back of a fork.

PEPPER RINGS WITH GOAT'S CHEESE

INGREDIENTS
2 large red or green peppers
1 onion, finely chopped
8oz (250g) tomatoes, chopped
2 tsp (10ml) chopped fresh basil
¼ tsp black pepper
4oz (125g) soft goat's cheese (or low- or medium-fat soft cheese)
4 tbsp (60ml) natural yogurt
•

NUTRITION PROFILE
This low-calorie dish is a good source of Vitamins A and C.

• Per portion •
Carbohydrate: 5.7g
Protein: 5.4g **Fibre:** 1.9g
Fat: 5.7g **Calories:** 95

Goat's cheese, or chèvre, is white with a crumbly texture and a clean, sharp taste. Choose one with a relatively mild flavour or use a low-fat curd cheese instead.

Preparation time: 20 mins   Cooking time: 40 mins
Serves 4

METHOD

1. Put the whole peppers under a preheated grill, turning them until the skin becomes crisp and blackened. Cool, then peel off the outer skin. Slice the peppers into ¾ inch (2cm) rings, removing any seeds.

2. Put the onion and tomatoes into the base of a large casserole or ovenproof dish. Sprinkle over the basil and pepper.

3. With a fork, mash together the goat's cheese and yogurt.

4. Arrange the pepper rings over the tomatoes and onion. Fill each with some of the cheese and yogurt mixture. Cover the casserole.

5. Bake in a preheated oven at Gas Mark 4, 350°F, 180°C for 30–40 minutes. Serve hot or cold.

Illustrated on page 46

RED CABBAGE WITH BEETROOT

INGREDIENTS

2 tsp (10ml) olive oil
12oz (350g) red cabbage, shredded
6oz (175g) raw beetroot, coarsely grated
1 large onion, finely chopped
1 clove garlic, crushed
2 tbsp (30ml) shoyu
1 tbsp (15ml) concentrated apple juice
3 tbsp (45ml) cider vinegar

•

NUTRITION PROFILE

This low-calorie recipe is a good source of Vitamin C and folic acid.

• Per portion •
Carbohydrate: 9g
Protein: 2.4g **Fibre:** 4.6g
Fat: 2.5g **Calories:** 70

With their complementary flavours and colour, beetroot and red cabbage make an attractive combination, especially when topped with a little natural yogurt. Try serving this as an accompaniment to egg dishes, such as a soufflé or an omelette.

Preparation time: 25 mins   Cooking time: 10 mins
Serves 4

METHOD

1. Heat the oil in a large frying pan. Cover and gently fry the cabbage, beetroot, onion and garlic for 10–15 minutes stirring frequently.

2. Mix the shoyu, concentrated apple juice and cider vinegar together. Pour over the vegetables. Continue cooking gently for a further 10 minutes. Serve hot or cold.

Illustrated opposite

MUSHROOMS BAKED WITH OREGANO

INGREDIENTS

8oz (250g) flat mushrooms
2 tbsp (30ml) lemon juice
1 tbsp (15ml) shoyu
1 tbsp (15ml) tomato purée
1 clove garlic, crushed
2 tsp (10ml) chopped fresh oregano
1/2 tsp black pepper
3 fl oz (75ml) water
1 tsp (5ml) olive oil

•

NUTRITION PROFILE

Low in calories and fat, this recipe is a good source of copper and niacin.

• Per portion •
Carbohydrate: 2.7g
Protein: 1.6g **Fibre:** 1.7g
Fat: 1.8g **Calories:** 35

Flat mushrooms are button mushrooms that have been allowed to develop and open their caps. Baked slowly in a well-flavoured stock, they make a delicious accompaniment to a vegetable risotto.

Preparation time: 10 mins   Cooking time: 30 mins
Serves 4

METHOD

1. Arrange the mushrooms in the base of a large casserole.

2. Mix together the lemon juice, shoyu, tomato purée, garlic, oregano, black pepper and water. Pour on to the mushrooms and brush lightly with the olive oil.

3. Cover the casserole and bake in a preheated oven at Gas Mark 4, 350°F, 180°C for 30 minutes. Serve hot or cold.

Illustrated opposite

Clockwise from top: **Pepper rings with goat's cheese** (*see p.45*); **Red cabbage with beetroot** (*see above*); **Mushrooms baked with oregano** (*see above*).

CELERY AND LEEKS IN SHERRY

INGREDIENTS

¼ tsp olive oil
6 sticks celery, cut into 1 inch
(2.5cm) slices
12oz (375g) leeks, cut into 1 inch
(2.5cm) slices
¼ pint (150ml) medium sherry
¼ tsp black pepper
1 tsp chopped fresh thyme
1 tsp (5ml) concentrated apple juice

•

NUTRITION PROFILE

*This low-fat and low-calorie recipe
contains a good quantity of Vitamin C.*

• Per portion •
Carbohydrate: 7.8g
Protein: 2g **Fibre:** 3.4g
Fat: 0.3g **Calories:** 85

This quickly prepared dish combines two vegetables that are both low in calories and high in fibre. The stock from the cooked celery and leeks could be drained off, and thickened with a little cornflour or arrowroot to make a delicious sauce. Serve this as a side dish or as a hot starter with garlic bread.

Preparation time: 10 mins   Cooking time: 1¼ hours
Serves 4

METHOD

1. Brush the oil around the inside of a casserole or ovenproof dish. Layer the celery and leeks in the casserole.

2. Mix together the sherry, pepper, thyme and concentrated apple juice. Pour over the celery and leeks. Cover the casserole.

3. Bake in a preheated oven at Gas Mark 5, 375°F, 190°C for 1¼ hours or until the vegetables are tender. Serve hot.

Illustrated opposite

MEDITERRANEAN POTATOES

INGREDIENTS

½ tsp olive oil
1½ lb (750g) potatoes, cut
into chunks
6 cloves garlic, chopped
¼ pint (150ml) red wine
1 tbsp (15ml) tomato purée
2½ fl oz (65ml) water
1 tsp (5ml) chopped fresh rosemary
1 tsp (5ml) chopped fresh oregano
2 tbsp (30ml) chopped fresh parsley
¼ tsp black pepper

•

NUTRITION PROFILE

*This low-fat dish is a good source of
Vitamins B₁, B₆ and C.*

• Per portion •
Carbohydrate: 45.4g
Protein: 5.3g **Fibre:** 4.7g
Fat: 1g **Calories:** 220

In this aromatic dish, the potatoes absorb the flavours of the herbs, garlic and red wine when they are cooked in the oven. If you prefer, replace the wine with 1 tbsp (15ml) red wine vinegar and ¼ pint (150ml) water.

Preparation time: 15 mins   Cooking time: 1¼ hours
Serves 4

METHOD

1. Brush a large ovenproof dish or casserole with the olive oil. Put in the potatoes and garlic.

2. Mix together the red wine, tomato purée, water, rosemary, oregano, parsley and pepper. Pour over the potatoes.

3. Cover and bake in a preheated oven at Gas Mark 5, 375°F, 190°C for 1¼ hours, or until the potatoes are tender. Serve hot.

Illustrated opposite

From top: **Carrots and dill** (*see p.50*); **Celery and leeks in sherry** (*see above*); **Mediterranean potatoes** (*see above*);
Red cabbage and apple (*see p.50*).

CARROTS AND DILL

INGREDIENTS

2 tsp (10ml) sunflower oil
1 large onion, sliced into fine rings
1 lb (500g) carrots, cut into fingers
1 tsp (5ml) dill seeds
1/2 tsp yeast extract
1/4 pint (150ml) hot water
salt and black pepper

•

NUTRITION PROFILE

This low-calorie recipe is rich in Vitamins A, C and E.

• Per portion •
Carbohydrate: 8.5g
Protein: 1.6g   **Fibre:** 4g
Fat: 2.7g   **Calories:** 60

The carrot is a nutritious vegetable. It contains a high concentration of carotene, which converts to Vitamin A in the body, and is richer in calcium and potassium than most other vegetables. Dill provides an exciting flavour that contrasts with sweet whole baby carrots, which are available in late spring and summer.

Preparation time: 20 mins   Cooking time: 10 mins
Serves 4

METHOD

1. Heat the oil in a saucepan and fry the onion rings, carrots and dill seeds for 5–10 minutes.

2. Dissolve the yeast extract in the hot water and pour over the carrots. Cover and cook gently for 10 minutes until the carrots are just tender, adding a little extra water if necessary. Season to taste and serve hot.

Illustrated on page 49

RED CABBAGE AND APPLE

INGREDIENTS

1 1/4 lb (625g) red cabbage, sliced
6oz (175g) pickling onions or shallots, cut in half
1 large clove garlic, chopped
12oz (375g) eating apples, cored and sliced
1 tsp (5ml) dill seeds
2 cloves
1oz (25g) sultanas
3 fl oz (75ml) cider vinegar
3 fl oz (75ml) water
1 tbsp (15ml) concentrated apple juice

•

NUTRITION PROFILE

This high-fibre vegetable dish is low in fat, and a good source of calcium, folic acid and Vitamin C.

• Per portion •
Carbohydrate: 25.1g
Protein: 3.6g   **Fibre:** 8.2g
Fat: 0.2g   **Calories:** 110

This traditional recipe is made slightly more unusual by the addition of sultanas and cloves. It is easy to prepare and with its slightly piquant flavour makes a good accompaniment to richer dishes like a loaf or a roast.

Preparation time: 10 mins   Cooking time: 1 1/4 hours
Serves 4

METHOD

1. Layer the cabbage, onion, garlic, apple, dill seeds, cloves and sultanas in a large casserole.

2. Mix together the cider vinegar, water and concentrated apple juice. Pour over the vegetables. Cover the casserole.

3. Bake in a preheated oven at Gas Mark 4, 350°F, 180°C for 1 1/4 hours. Serve hot or cold.

Illustrated on page 49

LOAVES AND ROASTS

Combinations of nuts, pulses and vegetables which are
then packed into moulds to make loaf- or wheel-shaped
dishes are not only good sources of protein and fibre, but
make attractive centrepieces, ideal for special occasions.
Serve with a sauce of a contrasting colour or a fresh, green
salad for a healthy, appetizing meal.

  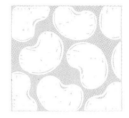

BLACK-EYED BEAN LOAF

INGREDIENTS

6oz (175g) black-eyed beans, soaked
2 tsp (10ml) sunflower oil
1 onion, finely chopped
2 cloves garlic, crushed
4oz (125g) unsalted peanuts, chopped
4oz (125g) wholemeal breadcrumbs
2 tbsp (30ml) sugar-free tomato
ketchup or tomato purée
2 tbsp (30ml) shoyu
2 tsp (10ml) chopped fresh basil
2 tsp (10ml) chopped fresh marjoram
2 large tomatoes, chopped
1 egg, beaten
3–4 tbsp (45–60ml) bean stock

•

NUTRITION PROFILE

*High in protein and fibre, this loaf is also
rich in Vitamins B$_1$, B$_6$, C and E, niacin,
magnesium, calcium, zinc, iron
and copper.*

• Per portion •
Carbohydrate: 44.8g
Protein: 23g   **Fibre:** 7.8g
Fat: 20.8g   **Calories:** 460

*Originating from California, black-eyed beans are small, ivory-
coloured and kidney-shaped with a black spot. To reduce the fat
content do not fry the garlic and onion. Serve with a tomato sauce
(see p. 65) and garnish with marjoram.*

Preparation time: 20 mins (plus 10–12 hours soaking time)
Cooking time: 40 mins (plus 40 mins for the beans)
Serves 4–6

METHOD

1. Drain the beans. Put in a saucepan and cover with fresh water.
Bring to the boil and boil fast for 10 minutes. Reduce the heat,
cover and simmer for 25–30 minutes until the beans are soft.
Drain, reserving the stock, and mash the beans.

2. Heat the oil in a pan and gently fry the onion and garlic for 5
minutes. Mix into the mashed beans, together with the peanuts,
breadcrumbs, tomato ketchup or purée, shoyu, basil and
marjoram. Gently stir in the tomatoes and the beaten egg. Add
sufficient bean stock to make a moist consistency.

3. Lightly oil a 1 lb (500g) loaf tin. Put the mixture into the tin
and press down well. Bake in a preheated oven at Gas Mark 4,
350°F, 180°C for 35–40 minutes. Leave in the tin for a few
minutes before turning out. Serve hot or cold.

Illustrated on page 52

HAZELNUT LOAF
WITH MUSHROOM AND PEPPER SAUCE

INGREDIENTS

4oz (125g) hazelnuts, ground
4oz (125g) wholemeal breadcrumbs
2 tsp (10ml) sunflower oil
1 onion, finely chopped
2 large carrots, grated
2 sticks celery, finely chopped
1 tsp (5ml) chopped fresh sage
1 tsp (5ml) chopped fresh thyme
1 tsp (5ml) yeast extract
$1/4$ pint (150ml) boiling water
1 tbsp (15ml) shoyu
1 egg, beaten
3 large tomatoes, sliced
3 tbsp (45ml) chopped fresh parsley

SAUCE

1oz (25g) vegetable margarine
2 tsp (10ml) chopped fresh dill
pinch chilli powder
4oz (125g) mushrooms, finely chopped
1 small green pepper, deseeded and
finely chopped
1oz (25g) wholemeal flour
$1/2$ pint (300ml) skimmed milk
2 tsp (10ml) shoyu

•

NUTRITION PROFILE

Vitamins A, B_1, C and E, magnesium and zinc are provided by this loaf. The sauce is rich in calcium, Vitamins B_2, C and D. Together they are high in fibre, protein and Vitamin B_{12}.

• Per portion •
Carbohydrate: 27.9g
Protein: 12.5g **Fibre:** 8.7g
Fat: 21.6g **Calories:** 355

This nut loaf makes a nutritious and satisfying meal, whether you serve it hot in the light, creamy sauce with steamed vegetables, or cold with a salad. The central layer of herbs and juicy tomatoes and the spicy mushroom and pepper sauce lend a piquant flavour and moisten the texture of the loaf. Garnish the loaf with a sprig of sage, and the sauce with a sprig of dill.

Preparation time: 25 mins   Cooking time: 40 mins
Serves 4

METHOD

1. Mix the hazelnuts and breadcrumbs together in a large bowl.

2. Heat the oil in a pan and gently fry the onion, carrots and celery for 5 minutes until soft. Add to the nut and breadcrumb mixture, together with the sage and thyme.

3. Dissolve the yeast extract in the water, and add to the bowl with the shoyu. Mix in the beaten egg.

4. Put about half the nut mixture into the base of a lightly oiled 1 lb (500g) loaf tin. Cover with the sliced tomatoes and parsley. Top with the rest of the nut mixture.

5. Bake in a preheated oven at Gas Mark 4, 350°F, 180°C for 35–40 minutes. Serve hot or cold.

6. For the sauce, melt the margarine in a small pan, add the dill and chilli powder, mushrooms and green pepper. Cover and cook gently for 10 minutes.

7. Stir in the flour and cook for 2–3 minutes. Remove from the heat and gradually stir in the milk. Bring to the boil, stirring continuously, and simmer gently for 3–4 minutes. Add the shoyu and serve.

Illustrated opposite

Top: **Black-eyed bean loaf** (*see p.51*); Bottom: **Hazelnut loaf with mushroom and pepper sauce** (*see above*).

CAULIFLOWER ~AND~ ALMOND BAKE

INGREDIENTS

1 medium cauliflower, cut into florets
2 tsp (10ml) sunflower oil
1 onion, chopped
1 clove garlic, crushed
2oz (50g) almonds, roughly chopped
2oz (50g) ground almonds
½ pint (300ml) water
1 tbsp (15ml) shoyu
1 tsp (5 ml) chopped fresh marjoram

•

NUTRITION PROFILE

This high-fibre dish provides Vitamins C and E, folic acid, magnesium and calcium.

• Per portion •
Carbohydrate: 4.9g
Protein: 6.9g **Fibre:** 6.5g
Fat: 15.9g **Calories:** 190

An interesting and healthy alternative to cauliflower cheese, this recipe combines lightly steamed cauliflower with almonds and herbs. Serve with brown rice or jacket potatoes and a green salad; garnish with lemon slices and parsley.

Preparation time: 35 mins   Cooking time: 30 mins
Serves 4

METHOD

1. Put the cauliflower into a steamer or colander over a pan of boiling water and steam gently for 10–15 minutes, until the cauliflower is just tender. Reserve the steaming water and make up to ½ pint (300ml) with fresh water. Put the cauliflower into the base of a large ovenproof dish.

2. Heat the oil in a pan and gently fry the onion and garlic for 5 minutes. Add the roughly chopped almonds and cook gently for a further 4–5 minutes. Spoon over the cauliflower.

3. In a blender or food processor, mix together the ground almonds, cauliflower water, shoyu and marjoram. Pour over the cauliflower. Bake in a preheated oven at Gas Mark 4, 350°F, 180°C for 25–30 minutes. Serve hot.

Illustrated opposite

CHEESE ~AND~ WALNUT LOAF

INGREDIENTS

8oz (250g) cottage cheese
2oz (50g) walnuts, ground
2 tsp (10ml) wholegrain mustard
4oz (125g) wholemeal breadcrumbs
8 black peppercorns, crushed
2 eggs, beaten

•

NUTRITION PROFILE

This high-protein loaf contains plenty of zinc and Vitamins B_2, B_{12} and D.

• Per portion •
Carbohydrate: 15.3g
Protein: 16.3g **Fibre:** 3.4g
Fat: 13.3g **Calories:** 240

This nutty loaf is ideal for serving with salads, green vegetables or with a tomato or mushroom sauce. For a smoother texture, try using low-fat curd cheese instead of cottage cheese. Garnish with curly endive.

Preparation time: 10 mins   Cooking time: 30–40 mins
Serves 4

METHOD

1. Combine the cottage cheese, walnuts, mustard, breadcrumbs, peppercorns and eggs in a large bowl and mix well.

2. Lightly oil a 1 lb (500g) loaf tin or a small casserole. Put the mixture into the tin or dish.

3. Bake in a preheated oven at Gas Mark 4, 350°F, 180°C for 30–40 minutes until golden brown. Serve hot or cold.

Illustrated opposite

Top: **Cheese and walnut loaf** (*see above*); Bottom: **Cauliflower and almond bake** (*see above*).

COLOURFUL PINTO LOAF
WITH CARROT SAUCE

INGREDIENTS

6oz (175g) pinto beans, soaked
2 tsp (10ml) olive oil
1 large onion, finely chopped
2 cloves garlic, crushed
4oz (125g) carrot, grated
6oz (175g) sweetcorn, fresh, frozen
or canned
1½ tsp (7.5ml) dill seeds
4 tsp (20ml) chopped fresh marjoram
4oz (125g) porridge oats
1 egg
2 tbsp (30ml) shoyu
¼ tsp black pepper
3–4 tbsp (45–60ml) bean stock
1 small red pepper, deseeded and cut
into thin strips
1small green pepper, deseeded and cut
into thin strips

SAUCE

2 tsp (10ml) olive oil
1 large onion, finely chopped
8oz (250g) carrots, sliced
¾ pint (450ml) vegetable stock
or water
1 tsp (5ml) yeast extract
4 tbsp (60ml) orange juice
2 tbsp (30ml) chopped fresh parsley

•

NUTRITION PROFILE

*This protein- and fibre-rich loaf is also high
in iron, magnesium, zinc, calcium, folic
acid and Vitamins A, B₁, B₆ and C. The
low-calorie sauce is rich in Vitamins
A and C.*

• Per portion •
Carbohydrate: 68.4g
Protein: 19.6g   **Fibre:** 10.9g
Fat: 10.4g   **Calories:** 445

*Speckled pinto beans make a high-protein loaf, which is delicious served
hot with a carrot sauce, or cold with a selection of salads. The sauce is
very versatile and would make an ideal accompaniment to a rice dish
or pasta.*

Preparation time: 30 mins (plus 10–12 hours soaking time)
Cooking time: 40 mins (plus 40 mins for the beans)
Serves 4–6

METHOD

1. Drain the beans. Place in a saucepan and cover with fresh water.
Bring to the boil and boil fast for 10 minutes. Reduce the heat,
cover and simmer for 30 minutes, or until the beans are soft. Drain,
reserving the stock, and mash the beans while still warm.

2. Heat the oil and gently fry the onion and garlic for 5–7
minutes. Add the carrot and sweetcorn. If using frozen sweetcorn,
defrost first; if using fresh sweetcorn, cook in boiling water for 5
minutes first. Rinse canned sweetcorn before using. Cook for a
further 5 minutes.

3. Stir in the dill seeds, marjoram, mashed beans and porridge
oats and mix well. Beat together the egg, shoyu and black pepper.
Add to the bean mixture. Add enough stock to make a
moist consistency.

4. Lightly oil a 2 lb (1kg) loaf tin. Lay half the strips of red and
green pepper along the base. Top with half of the bean mixture.
Then lay the rest of the pepper strips on top, finishing with the
remaining bean mixture.

5. Bake in a preheated oven at Gas Mark 4, 350°F, 180°C for
35–40 minutes. Leave in the tin for 5 minutes before turning out.

6. For the sauce, heat the oil in a pan and gently fry the onion for
5–7 minutes. Add the carrots and cook for a further 2–3 minutes.

7. Pour on the water or vegetable stock, add the yeast extract.
Bring to the boil, cover and simmer for 10 minutes, until the
carrots are tender. Remove from the heat. Cool slightly.

8. Purée the vegetables in a blender or food processor until
smooth. Return to the pan, add the orange juice and parsley.
Warm through gently, check the seasoning and serve on top of
the loaf.

Illustrated opposite

Top: **Colourful pinto loaf with carrot sauce** (*see above*); Bottom: **Almond wheel** (*see p.58*).

ALMOND WHEEL

INGREDIENTS

2 tsp (10ml) olive oil
1 large onion, finely chopped
1 clove garlic, crushed
8oz (250g) long-grain brown rice
3oz (75g) blanched almonds, chopped
1 yellow pepper, deseeded and chopped
2oz (50g) raisins
1 tsp (5ml) ground cinnamon
grated rind of 1 orange
3 tbsp (45ml) orange juice
1 tbsp (15ml) shoyu
1 tbsp (15ml) tahini

FILLING

12oz (375g) tomatoes, chopped
6oz (175g) French beans, trimmed
1 clove garlic, crushed
1 tsp (5ml) chopped fresh basil
2 tbsp (30ml) chopped fresh parsley

•

NUTRITION PROFILE

This high-fibre recipe supplies Vitamins A, B₁, B₂, C and E, niacin, folic acid, zinc, magnesium, copper, calcium and iron.

• Per portion •
Carbohydrate: 68.2g
Protein: 10.8g   **Fibre:** 10g
Fat: 16.9g   **Calories:** 455

This summery combination is ideal for a special occasion or buffet. Make sure the vegetables are lightly cooked and still crunchy.

Preparation time: 1 hour   Cooking time: 30 mins
Serves 4

METHOD

1. Heat the oil in a large pan and gently fry the onion and garlic for 5 minutes. Add the rice and almonds, and cook gently for 3–4 minutes until the almonds begin to turn golden brown.

2. Add the yellow pepper, raisins and cinnamon and cook for 2–3 minutes. Stir in the orange rind, juice and 1 pint (600ml) boiling water. Bring to the boil, cover and simmer for 30 minutes. Drain and stir in the shoyu and tahini.

3. Lightly oil an 8 inch (20cm) ring mould and press the rice mixture into the mould (see below). Bake in a preheated oven at Gas Mark 4, 350°F, 180°C for 30 minutes, or until firm.

4. For the filling, gently cook the tomatoes for 5 minutes. Stir in the French beans, garlic, basil and parsley. Cover and cook for 8–10 minutes. Add a little water if the mixture seems dry.

5. Turn out the rice. Fill the centre of the ring with the tomatoes and beans. Serve hot or cold.

Illustrated on page 57

USING A RING MOULD

The shape of a dish can often be an important part of its appeal, just as much as its colour, texture and aroma. Ring moulds are used to make circular loaves and cakes, as well as mousses and jellies. If you do not have a ring mould, an upside down mixing bowl and a loose-bottomed cake tin will do just as well.

1. If using a mould, brush the sides with a little oil, tightly pack in the mixture and bake.

2. If making your own mould, line a cake tin and place a pyrex bowl in the centre. Brush with a little oil.

3. When baked, turn out onto a plate, and remove the cake tin, greaseproof paper and finally the bowl.

GRAINS AND ~ PASTA

Grains and pasta, both excellent sources of fibre, B Vitamins and protein, have long been staple foods. They combine well with nuts, seeds, pulses and vegetables, and, served with a sauce, make a substantial, healthy dish which is also easy to prepare.

WINTER VEGETABLES WITH BUCKWHEAT

INGREDIENTS

2 tsp (10ml) sunflower oil
6oz (175g) unroasted buckwheat
4oz (125g) red split lentils
1 large onion, finely chopped
1 clove garlic, crushed
6oz (175g) carrots, thinly sliced
8oz (250g) leeks, finely sliced
6oz (175g) parsnips, grated
2 tsp (10ml) chopped fresh rosemary
1 tsp (5ml) chopped fresh thyme
1 pint (600ml) boiling water
2 tbsp (30ml) shoyu
3 tbsp (45ml) tahini

•

NUTRITION PROFILE

This casserole contains Vitamins A, C and E and niacin, iron, zinc, calcium and magnesium.

• Per portion •
Carbohydrate: 58.8g
Protein: 18.8g **Fibre:** 13.5g
Fat: 11.3g **Calories:** 410

Buckwheat is a tasty and nutritious grain, available roasted or unroasted. If you are using ready-roasted buckwheat, simply put the oil in the pan with the buckwheat and lentils and move straight on to step 2. If you are using lentils that have not been ready-prepared, remember to rinse them well and pick over for stones. This dish can be served as a slice or as a loaf and then turned out. Serve hot with a mushroom or tomato sauce, or cold with salads.

Preparation time: 35 mins   Cooking time: 25–45 mins
Serves 4

METHOD

1. Heat the oil over a moderate heat and gently cook the buckwheat and lentils for 5 minutes to lightly toast the buckwheat.

2. Add the onion and garlic and fry for 3 minutes. Add the carrots, leeks and parsnips, rosemary and thyme and cook for 5 minutes.

3. Add the boiling water, cover and simmer for 15 minutes. Stir in the shoyu and tahini. Check the seasoning.

4. Put the mixture into a lightly oiled 12 × 8 inch (30 × 20cm) tin or a lined 1 lb (500g) loaf tin. Bake in a preheated oven at Gas Mark 4, 350°F, 180°C for 25 minutes if using a rectangular tin, or 45 minutes if using the loaf tin. Serve hot or cold.

Illustrated on page 60

HARVEST HOT POT

INGREDIENTS

8oz (250g) wheat grain
2 tsp (10ml) sunflower oil
8oz (250g) shallots, peeled
2 small leeks, trimmed and sliced
1 large potato, diced
6oz (175g) carrots, sliced
6oz (175g) button mushrooms
2 tsp (10ml) chopped fresh rosemary
2 tsp (10ml) chopped fresh thyme
1 tsp (5ml) yeast extract

•

NUTRITION PROFILE

This dish is a good source of iron, zinc, calcium, copper, folic acid and Vitamins A, B_1, B_2, B_6, C and E.

• Per portion •
Carbohydrate: 57.5g
Protein: 12.1g **Fibre:** 11.2g
Fat: 4.3g **Calories:** 300

Wheat grain is sometimes referred to as wholewheat berries. It makes a nutritious and interesting alternative to rice. Serve with a green vegetable and a sprig of thyme to garnish.

Preparation time: 45 mins   Cooking time: 30 mins
Serves 4

METHOD

1. Cover the wheat grain with plenty of water. Bring to the boil, cover and simmer for 30 minutes. Drain and reserve the stock.

2. Heat the oil in a large pan and gently fry the shallots, leeks, potato, carrots and mushrooms for 8–10 minutes. Add the rosemary, thyme and cooked wheat grain.

3. Make the reserved stock up to $3/4$ pint (450ml) with water. Add to the wheat and vegetables together with the yeast extract. Bring to the boil, cover and simmer for 30 minutes. Serve hot.

Illustrated opposite

SUMMER VEGETABLES WITH GOLDEN MILLET

INGREDIENTS

2 tsp (10ml) sunflower oil
6oz (175g) millet
1 bunch spring onions, chopped
1 small green pepper, chopped
6oz (175g) courgettes, thickly sliced
4oz (125g) French beans, cut into
1 inch (2.5cm) pieces
$1/2$ pint (300ml) apple juice
$1/2$ pint (300ml) boiling water
2 tsp (10ml) chopped fresh thyme
grated rind of 1 large lemon
2oz (50g) blanched almonds
4 medium tomatoes, cut into quarters

•

NUTRITION PROFILE

This low-fat, high-protein, high-fibre recipe is rich in Vitamins B_1, B_2, C and E and in folic acid, calcium and iron.

• Per portion •
Carbohydrate: 57.5g
Protein: 6.6g **Fibre:** 7.2g
Fat: 10.3g **Calories:** 305

Golden-coloured millet is a nutritious grain. Here it combines perfectly with summer vegetables, which could be altered according to availability. Garnish with tomato slices.

Preparation time: 30 mins   Cooking time: 20 mins
Serves 4

METHOD

1. Heat the oil in a large pan and lightly toast the millet until it starts to become golden brown. Add the spring onions, pepper, courgettes and French beans and cook gently for 5–7 minutes.

2. Stir in the apple juice, boiling water, thyme and lemon rind. Bring to the boil, cover and simmer gently for 15–20 minutes until the millet is cooked.

3. Meanwhile toast the almonds under a preheated moderate grill, or in a preheated oven at Gas Mark 4, 350°F, 180°C for 4–5 minutes until golden brown. Roughly chop the toasted almonds.

4. Add the almonds and tomatoes to the millet. Serve hot or cold.

Illustrated opposite

Clockwise from top: **Winter vegetables with buckwheat** (*see p.59*); **Harvest hot pot** (*see above*); **Summer vegetables with golden millet** (*see above*).

ALMOND $\underset{\sim}{AND}$ VEGETABLE PAELLA

INGREDIENTS

2 tsp (10ml) sunflower oil
1 onion, chopped
1 clove garlic, crushed
3oz (75g) whole almonds, blanched
6oz (175g) long-grain brown rice
1 stick celery, chopped
8oz (250g) summer green vegetables
1 small green pepper, sliced into strips
1 tsp (5ml) cumin seeds, crushed
2 tsp (10ml) chopped fresh marjoram
1 tbsp (15ml) shoyu or salt and pepper

•

NUTRITION PROFILE

*This dish is rich in Vitamins B_1, C and E,
iron, magnesium and folic acid.*

• Per portion •
Carbohydrate: 47.9g
Protein: 11.8g   **Fibre:** 6.4g
Fat: 4.5g   **Calories:** 360

*This combination of nuts, vegetables and rice makes an easily prepared
meal. Brown rice is a good source of B vitamins and fibre, while
almonds not only provide protein, but also give a creamy flavour.*

Preparation time: 20 mins   Cooking time: 30 mins
Serves 4

METHOD

1. Heat the oil in a large pan and fry the onion and garlic for 5
minutes. Add the almonds and rice and cook for 5 minutes. Add
the celery, green vegetables, green pepper, cumin seeds and
marjoram. Cook gently for a further 5 minutes.

2. Stir in 2 bay leaves and 1 pint (600ml) boiling water. Bring to
the boil, cover and simmer for 30 minutes until the rice is cooked
and the liquid has been absorbed.

3. Add the shoyu, or season with salt and pepper, add 1 tbsp
(15ml) lemon juice, remove the bay leaves and serve hot.

Illustrated opposite

AUBERGINE $\underset{\sim}{AND}$ MUSHROOM RICE

INGREDIENTS

8oz (250g) long-grain brown rice
2 tsp (10ml) olive oil
1 large onion, chopped
1 large clove garlic, chopped
12oz (375g) aubergine, diced
4oz (125g) mushrooms, quartered
2 tsp (10ml) chopped fresh marjoram
2 tsp (10ml) chopped fresh thyme
1 tsp (5ml) paprika
1oz (25g) wholemeal or soya flour
½ pint (300ml) skimmed milk
1 tbsp (15ml) shoyu

•

NUTRITION PROFILE

*This dish provides magnesium, zinc,
copper, calcium, iron, folic acid, Vitamins
B_1, B_2, B_{12}, and C.*

• Per portion •
Carbohydrate: 64.7g
Protein: 10g   **Fibre:** 6.7g
Fat: 6.2g   **Calories:** 340

*This dish is topped with a creamy vegetable sauce made with soya flour.
It is excellent served with broccoli or tomatoes.*

Preparation time: 1 hour   Cooking time: 30 mins
Serves 4

METHOD

1. Place the rice in 1 pint (600ml) boiling water. Bring to the
boil, cover and simmer for 25 minutes. Drain and transfer the rice
to a large casserole or ovenproof dish.

2. Heat the oil and gently fry the onion and garlic for 5 minutes. Add
the aubergine and mushrooms and cook for a further 10 minutes.

3. Add the marjoram, thyme, paprika and flour and cook for 2–3
minutes. Add the milk and simmer gently for 5 minutes. Add the
shoyu and check the seasoning.

4. Put the aubergine mixture on top of the rice. Sprinkle with
sesame seeds if you like. Cover and bake in a preheated oven at
Gas Mark 4, 350°F, 180°C for 30 minutes. Serve hot.

Illustrated opposite

Clockwise from top: **Almond and vegetable paella** (*see above*); **Aubergine and mushroom rice** (*see above*);
Sharp rice with mild sauce (*see p.64*).

SHARP RICE WITH MILD SAUCE

INGREDIENTS

1 tsp (5ml) sunflower oil
1 onion, finely chopped
1 small green pepper, deseeded
and diced
8oz (250g) long-grain brown rice
1 pint (600ml) boiling water
1 tsp (5ml) chopped fresh thyme
grated rind of 1 large lemon
¼ tsp salt

SAUCE

½ tsp sunflower oil
2 large leeks, finely chopped
2oz (50g) unsalted cashew nuts
2oz (50g) unsalted cashew nuts, ground
¼ pint (150ml) water
1 tbsp (15ml) shoyu

•

NUTRITION PROFILE

*This high-fibre dish is a good source of
Vitamins B₁, and C. It also contains
niacin, copper, magnesium and iron.*

• Per portion •
Carbohydrate: 62.8g
Protein: 10g **Fibre:** 6.1g
Fat: 15.2g **Calories:** 410

*This unusual dish has a tangy base of lemon-flavoured rice and is
topped with a smooth leek and cashew nut sauce. The contrasts of
flavour and texture make it an interesting recipe for a dinner party,
served with an endive salad, steamed spinach or sorrel.*

Preparation time: 25 mins   Cooking time: 30 mins
Serves 4

METHOD

1. Heat the oil over a moderate heat in a large pan and gently fry
the onion for 10 minutes. Add the pepper and rice and cook for a
further 5 minutes.

2. Pour on the water and stir in the thyme and lemon rind. Bring
to the boil, cover and simmer for 30 minutes, or until the rice is
cooked and the liquid absorbed. Season with the salt to taste.

3. For the sauce, heat the remaining oil in a large pan and gently
fry the leeks and the whole cashews, covered, for 15 minutes until
the cashews become golden brown.

4. Combine the ground cashews and water (see below), and then
pour on to the leeks and cashew nuts, and warm through gently.
Add a little extra water if necessary, to make a thick sauce. Add
the shoyu and check the seasoning.

5. Serve the rice hot, topped with the leek and cashew sauce.

Illustrated on page 63

MAKING NUT CREAM

*A nut-and-water sauce is quick to make, nutritious, full of flavour and extremely versatile as a base for
soups, mousses, soufflées and casseroles. Made to a thicker consistency and sweetened with a little honey,
nut creams are a marvellous topping for desserts and puddings.*

1. Place ground cashews in a blender or
food processor with ¼ pint (150ml)
water. Blend to a smooth liquid.

2. Add the nut-and-water mixture to
the other sauce ingredients as specified
in the recipe you are using (see above).

3. When the sauce is warmed through,
dilute to the required consistency.
Serve with rice.

WHOLEMEAL SPAGHETTI BAKE

INGREDIENTS

2 tsp (10ml) olive oil
1 onion, finely chopped
1 clove garlic, crushed
4oz (125g) mushrooms, sliced
1 eating apple, cored and grated
14oz (400g) can of chopped tomatoes
1 tsp (5ml) chopped fresh sage
2 tbsp (30ml) tomato purée
8oz (250g) wholemeal spaghetti
2oz (50g) Cheddar cheese, grated

•

NUTRITION PROFILE

This high-protein meal is rich in Vitamins A, C, niacin, folic acid, iron, copper and calcium.

• Per portion •
Carbohydrate: 47.8g
Protein: 14.5g **Fibre:** 9.4g
Fat: 7.9g **Calories:** 320

Wholemeal spaghetti contains more nutrients and fibre than ordinary pasta and combines with herbs and tomatoes to make a satisfying lunch or supper dish. If you wish to assemble the recipe in advance and bake it in the oven just before serving, add a little extra tomato juice to the sauce, as the consistency of the dish becomes thicker on standing.

Preparation time: 40 mins   Cooking time: 25 mins
Serves 4

METHOD

1. Heat the oil in a large pan and gently fry the onion and garlic for 5 minutes.

2. Add the mushrooms, cover and cook for a further 5 minutes.

3. Stir in the apple. Drain the tomatoes, reserving the juice. Add the tomatoes to the pan with the sage and tomato purée. Cover and simmer gently for 10 minutes, adding a little tomato juice or water to make a thick sauce, if necessary.

4. Meanwhile, cook the spaghetti in a saucepan of boiling water for 5–7 minutes until it is just tender. Drain.

5. Mix the sauce and spaghetti together and put into a large casserole or ovenproof dish. Sprinkle over the cheese.

6. Bake in a preheated oven at Gas Mark 4, 350°F, 180°C for 20–25 minutes until golden brown and bubbling.

Illustrated on page 66

RED LENTIL LASAGNE

INGREDIENTS

2 tsp (10ml) olive oil
1 large onion, chopped
1 clove garlic, crushed
1 red or green pepper, deseeded
and chopped
4oz (125g) mushrooms, thickly sliced
2 tsp (10ml) chopped fresh basil
2 tsp (10ml) chopped fresh oregano
8oz (250g) red split lentils
14oz (400g) can of chopped tomatoes
$4^{1}/_{2}$–5 pints (2400–3000ml) water
1 bay leaf
1 tbsp (15ml) shoyu or salt and pepper
4oz (125g) wholemeal lasagne
(approximately 8 sheets)
1oz (25g) vegetable margarine
1oz (25g) wholemeal flour
$^{1}/_{2}$ pint (300ml) skimmed milk
$^{1}/_{2}$ tsp mustard powder
3oz (75g) Cheddar cheese, grated

•

NUTRITION PROFILE

*This is rich in iron, zinc, copper, calcium,
magnesium and folic acid; also niacin,
Vitamins A, B_1, B_2, C, D, protein
and fibre.*

• Per portion •
Carbohydrate: 66.4g
Protein: 29.3g **Fibre:** 11.4g
Fat: 37.2g **Calories:** 700

*Various types of lasagne are available including stoneground,
wholemeal, spinach-flavoured and those which do not require pre-
cooking. Fresh lasagne is now on sale in many stores – or you can make
your own. If you use lasagne that does not need pre-cooking you will
need to add extra liquid to the lentil sauce and cook according to the
directions on the lasagne packet.*

Preparation time: $1^{1}/_{4}$ hours   Cooking time: 35 mins
Serves 4–6

METHOD

1. Heat the oil in a large pan and gently fry the onion and garlic
over a moderate heat for 5 minutes. Add the pepper and
mushrooms and cook for 5 minutes. Add the basil, oregano and
lentils, and cook gently for 2–3 minutes. Stir in the tomatoes and
their juice with $^{1}/_{2}$ pint (300ml) of the water and the bay leaf.

2. Bring to the boil, cover, and simmer for 20–25 minutes until
the lentils are soft. Add a little extra water if the mixture seems
too dry. Season with shoyu or salt and pepper, then remove
the bay leaf.

3. Meanwhile, put the lasagne into a large saucepan of boiling
water and simmer for 8–10 minutes until just tender. Drain, put
into a bowl and cover with cold water to keep the sheets pliant.

4. Melt the margarine in a small pan and stir in the flour. Cook
over a gentle heat for 3–4 minutes, stirring. Remove from the
heat and gradually stir in the milk. Bring to the boil, stirring all
the time, until the sauce thickens. Cook gently for 3–4 minutes,
stirring. Remove from the heat and beat in the mustard powder
and most of the cheese, reserving just a little to sprinkle on the
top. Check the seasoning.

5. Put a third of the lentil mixture into the base of a deep
casserole or ovenproof dish. Cover with a third of the lasagne,
then add another third of the lentils, followed by another third of
the lasagne. Cover this with half of the cheese sauce, then with
the rest of the lentils. Top with the remaining lasagne. Pour the
rest of the cheese sauce over the top, sprinkle with the cheese.

6. Bake in a preheated oven at Gas Mark 4, 350°F, 180°C for
30–35 minutes until bubbling and golden brown. Serve hot.

Illustrated opposite

Top: **Red lentil lasagne** (*see above*); Bottom: **Wholemeal spaghetti bake** (*see p. 65*).

CHILLI POLENTA
WITH SPICY MUSHROOM SAUCE

Polenta is a traditional Italian dish made with golden cornmeal. In this version the polenta is baked in the oven at a high temperature instead of fried. It is served with a spicy mushroom sauce and garnished with tomato. When using fresh chillis, do not include the stalk end and the seeds, unless you like the sauce really hot!

Preparation time: 1¼ hours   Cooking time: 15 mins
Serves 4

INGREDIENTS

½ pint (300ml) skimmed milk
½ pint (300ml) water
1 bay leaf
12 black peppercorns
1 clove garlic, roughly chopped
4oz (125g) coarse cornmeal
½ tsp olive oil
2 tbsp (30ml) grated Parmesan cheese

SAUCE
2 tsp (10ml) olive oil
1 large onion, chopped
1 clove garlic, crushed
1 fresh red chilli, deseeded
and chopped
4oz (125g) mushrooms, sliced
2 tsp (10ml) paprika
2 tsp (10ml) chopped fresh thyme
14oz (400g) can of chopped tomatoes

NUTRITION PROFILE

This dish is a good source of calcium and Vitamins A, B_2, B_{12} and C.

• Per portion •
Carbohydrate: 32.2g
Protein: 9.1g   Fibre: 3.9g
Fat: 5.7g   Calories: 215

METHOD

1. To make the polenta dough, put the milk, water, bay leaf, peppercorns and garlic in a small pan, and bring to the boil. Remove from the heat, cover and leave to stand for 20 minutes.

2. Strain into a jug. In a small bowl, mix a little of the strained milk mixture with the cornmeal to make a smooth paste. Gradually stir in the rest of the milk mixture. Return to the pan, bring to the boil and simmer for 10 minutes, stirring continuously.

3. Pour the polenta on to a greased baking tray and spread out to ½ inch (1cm) thickness. Set aside to cool.

4. For the sauce, heat the oil in a medium pan and gently fry the onion and garlic for 5 minutes. Add the chilli, mushrooms, paprika and thyme, and continue cooking for 5 minutes.

5. Drain the tomatoes, reserving the juice, and add to the onion mixture. Bring to the boil, cover and simmer for 25–30 minutes, adding a little extra tomato juice or water if necessary. Check the seasoning.

6. Cut the cold polenta into rounds or squares. Lightly oil a casserole or ovenproof dish and lay the polenta shapes in the dish so that they overlap. Sprinkle with the cheese. Bake in a preheated oven at Gas Mark 6, 400°F, 200°C for 15 minutes. Serve hot with the spicy mushroom sauce.

Illustrated opposite

Chilli polenta with spicy mushroom sauce (*see above*).

WHOLEMEAL MACARONI CHEESE
WITH FENNEL

INGREDIENTS

6oz (175g) wholemeal macaroni
½ pint (300ml) skimmed milk
½ onion
1 bay leaf
1½oz (40g) vegetable margarine
1oz (25g) wholemeal flour
2 tbsp (30ml) chopped chives or spring
onion tops
½ tsp black pepper
½ tsp yeast extract
1 head fennel, roughly chopped
2oz (50g) Cheddar cheese, grated

•

NUTRITION PROFILE

*This high-protein, high-fibre dish is also a
good source of iron, niacin and calcium
and Vitamins A, B₁, B₂, B₁₂ and D.*

• Per portion •
Carbohydrate: 45.6g
Protein: 14.3g **Fibre:** 7.7g
Fat: 13.3g **Calories:** 350

*This is a healthy version of the classic macaroni cheese, using
wholemeal pasta, skimmed milk and only a little cheese, to keep the fat
content down. Pasta and cheese together are a good source of protein.
The addition of raw fennel towards the end of the cooking time gives a
contrasting crunchy texture to the dish. Serve with a salad or
green vegetables.*

Preparation time: 40 mins   Cooking time: 25 mins
Serves 4

METHOD

1. Cook the macaroni in a saucepan of boiling water for 7–10
minutes until just tender. Drain well.

2. Heat the milk, onion and bay leaf in a small saucepan. Bring to
the boil, remove from the heat and allow the milk to infuse for
10 minutes.

3. Melt the margarine over a moderate heat in a small pan. Stir in
the flour and cook gently for 3–4 minutes to form a soft roux.

4. Remove the onion and bay leaf from the milk. Gradually add
the milk to the roux, stirring constantly. Bring to the boil over a
moderate heat, stirring well as the sauce thickens.

5. Stir in the chives, black pepper, yeast extract, cooked
macaroni and chopped fennel. Check the seasoning and cook for
2–3 minutes.

6. Transfer the mixture to a casserole or ovenproof dish and top
with the grated cheese. Bake in a preheated oven at Gas Mark 5,
375°F, 190°C for 25 minutes until golden brown. Alternatively,
cook under a preheated moderate grill for 10–15 minutes.
Serve hot garnished with fennel fronds.

Illustrated opposite

Wholemeal macaroni cheese with fennel (*see above*).

NUTS ᴀɴᴅ FRUITS

Nuts have an important role to play in healthy eating and are much more than a garnish. A rich source of B Vitamins, minerals, protein and fibre, they are delicious in savoury and sweet dishes. Fruit and nuts go particularly well together, as the flavours, textures and colours are so complementary.

SMOOTH ᴀɴᴅ CRUNCHY COURGETTES

INGREDIENTS

2 tsp (10ml) sunflower oil
1 lb (500g) courgettes, sliced
2 cloves garlic, crushed
4oz (125g) mushrooms, sliced
1 tsp (5ml) chopped fresh basil
14oz (400g) can of chopped tomatoes
2oz (50g) bulgar wheat
2oz (50g) unsalted cashew nuts
¼ pint (150ml) smetana or
natural yogurt

•

NUTRITION PROFILE

This high-fibre recipe is rich in iron, magnesium, copper, calcium, folic acid, niacin and Vitamins A, B_1, B_2, C and E.

• Per portion •
Carbohydrate: 26.1g
Protein: 10.2g   **Fibre:** 6.5g
Fat: 9.5g   **Calories:** 225

Smetana, a cultured skimmed milk product, is low in fat, yet creamy and full of flavour. Here it is used to make a delicious combination with courgettes, cashew nuts and bulgar wheat. This kind of wheat is made from whole grains that have been soaked and then baked until they crack into small yellow particles.

Preparation time: 15 mins   Cooking time: 10 mins
Serves 4

METHOD

1. Heat the oil in a large frying pan and gently fry the courgettes and garlic for 5 minutes. Add the mushrooms, cover and cook for 5 minutes.

2. Stir in the basil, tomatoes, bulgar wheat and cashew nuts. Cover and cook for a further 10 minutes.

3. Stir in the smetana or yogurt, warm through gently and serve hot.

Illustrated on page 74

SWEET ~^{AND} SOUR HAZELNUTS

INGREDIENTS

RISSOLES
4oz (125g) hazelnuts, ground
4oz (125g) wholemeal breadcrumbs
1 onion, finely chopped
1 clove garlic, crushed
2 tsp (10ml) mixed fresh herbs
1 tsp (5ml) yeast extract
1/4 pint (150ml) boiling water
1 egg, beaten
5 tbsp (75ml) wholemeal flour or
wholemeal breadcrumbs
1 tsp (5ml) sunflower oil

SAUCE
2 tsp (10ml) sunflower oil
4oz (125g) celery, trimmed and cut
into sticks
4oz (125g) carrots, cut into sticks
1 red pepper, deseeded and cut
into strips
1/2 pint (300ml) water
2 tbsp (30ml) arrowroot
1 tbsp (15ml) shoyu
1 tbsp (15ml) cider vinegar
1 tbsp (15ml) concentrated apple juice
2 tbsp (30ml) tomato purée

•

NUTRITION PROFILE

*This dish is an excellent source of Vitamins
A, B_1, B_6, B_12, C and E, magnesium,
iron, zinc, folic acid and fibre.*

• Per portion •
Carbohydrate: 33.5g
Protein: 10.4g   **Fibre:** 8g
Fat: 17.6g   **Calories:** 330

*Small rissoles made from hazelnuts and herbs are served here in a
delicious sweet and sour sauce. The rissoles could be fried, but for a
healthier dish, bake them in the oven. Serve with rice or jacket potatoes
and a crisp, green salad.*

Preparation time: 40 mins   Cooking time: 20 mins
Serves 4

METHOD

1. Mix together the hazelnuts, breadcrumbs, onion, garlic and
mixed herbs in a large bowl.

2. Dissolve the yeast extract in the boiling water and add to the
hazelnut mixture to give a moist consistency.

3. Divide the mixture into 12 small rissoles. Dip each one into
the beaten egg and then into the flour or breadcrumbs. Put the
rissoles on a lightly greased baking tray.

4. Bake in a preheated oven at Gas Mark 5, 375°F, 190°C for 20
minutes, turning once during the cooking time.

5. For the sauce, heat the oil in a medium pan and gently cook
the celery, carrots and pepper for 10 minutes.

6. In a bowl, mix a little of the water with the arrowroot to form a
thick paste and stir in the rest of the water. Add the shoyu, cider
vinegar, concentrated apple juice and tomato purée. Mix well.

7. Pour the tomato mixture over the vegetables. Bring to the boil,
stirring all the time. Continue cooking until the sauce thickens
and becomes clear. Simmer gently for a further 5–10 minutes
until the vegetables are just tender.

8. Add the hazelnut rissoles to the sauce, warm through gently
and serve garnished with celery leaves.

Illustrated on page 74

CASHEW NUT MOUSSAKA

INGREDIENTS

1 large aubergine, thinly sliced
2 tsp (10ml) olive oil
1 onion, chopped
1 clove garlic, crushed
4oz (125g) mushrooms, sliced
1 green pepper, deseeded and sliced
2oz (50g) unsalted cashew nuts,
    roughly chopped if large
1oz (25g) wholemeal breadcrumbs
1 tbsp (15ml) tomato purée
2 tsp (10ml) chopped fresh basil
1 tbsp (15ml) shoyu
$\frac{1}{4}$ pint (150ml) water
1oz (25g) wholemeal flour
$\frac{1}{2}$ pint (300ml) skimmed milk
1 egg
2oz (50g) Cheddar cheese, grated
salt and black pepper
2 tsp (10ml) grated Parmesan cheese

•

NUTRITION PROFILE

*This recipe is high in protein, calcium,
magnesium and Vitamins B_2, B_{12} and C.*

• Per portion •
Carbohydrate: 18.7g
Protein: 14g **Fibre:** 4.2g
Fat: 15.6g **Calories:** 265

*Traditionally, moussakas are very high in fat, because aubergines
absorb a lot of oil in cooking. However, here they are baked in very
little oil, and the white sauce is made without any fat.*

Preparation time: 50 mins   Cooking time: 40 mins
Serves 4

METHOD

1. Put the aubergine slices on to a large baking tray which has
been lightly brushed with $\frac{1}{2}$ teaspoon of the oil. Brush the tops of
the aubergine slices with another $\frac{1}{2}$ teaspoon of the oil. Bake in a
preheated oven at Gas Mark 5, 375°F, 190°C for 10 minutes.
Remove from the oven and set aside.

2. Heat the remaining oil in a large frying pan and gently fry the
onion and garlic for 4–5 minutes. Add the mushrooms and
pepper, cover and cook gently for a further 10 minutes.

3. Stir in the cashew nuts, breadcrumbs, tomato purée, basil,
shoyu and sufficient water to make a moist mixture. Check
the seasoning.

4. Put approximately half the onion and nut mixture into the base
of a large casserole or ovenproof dish. Top with half of the
aubergine slices. Then put in the remaining onion mixture and
cover with the rest of the aubergine slices.

5. Mix the flour, milk and egg in a blender or food processor until
smooth. Alternatively, put the flour into a large bowl, beat the
egg with the milk, then gradually beat into the flour.

6. Put the milk mixture into a small pan and slowly bring to the
boil, stirring continuously. Simmer for 3–4 minutes until
thickened, stirring continuously. Remove from the heat and stir
in the Cheddar cheese. Check the seasoning.

7. Pour the cheese sauce over the aubergine mixture. Sprinkle
with Parmesan cheese. Cover the dish.

8. Bake in the oven for 35–40 minutes, uncovered for the last
10 minutes. Serve hot garnished with tomato segments.

Illustrated opposite

Clockwise from top: **Smooth and crunchy courgettes** (*see p.72*); **Sweet and sour hazelnuts** (*see p.73*);
Cashew nut moussaka (*see above*).

CHESTNUT ~ MUSHROOM BAKE

INGREDIENTS

6oz (175g) dried chestnuts
1 pint (600ml) water
1 tsp (5ml) olive oil
1 clove garlic, crushed
6oz (175g) shallots or pickling onions,
peeled and sliced if large
6oz (175g) button mushrooms
4oz (125g) carrots, grated
1 stick celery, trimmed and
finely shredded
1 tsp (5ml) chopped fresh rosemary
1 tsp (5ml) chopped fresh thyme
1 tsp (5ml) chopped fresh sage
1 tbsp (15ml) shoyu
$1/4$ tsp black pepper

•

NUTRITION PROFILE

This low-calorie recipe is a good source of
fibre and Vitamins A, B_2 and C.

• Per portion •
Carbohydrate: 21g
Protein: 2.8g   **Fibre:** 5.7g
Fat: 2.8g   **Calories:** 115

Lower in calories than most nuts, dried chestnuts are now readily
available all year round, and are very easy to cook. Serve this unusual,
highly flavoured nut and vegetable dish with a sharp tomato sauce (see
p. 65) and jacket potatoes or salad. Garnish with celery leaves, carrot
slices and thyme.

Preparation time: $1^{1}/4$ hours   Cooking time: 40 mins
Serves 4

METHOD

1. Put the chestnuts into a large saucepan and pour over the
water. Bring to the boil, cover and simmer for 45 minutes or until
soft. Drain, reserve the stock, and mash the chestnuts or grind in
a blender or food processor.

2. Meanwhile, heat the oil in a large pan and gently fry the garlic
and shallots over a moderate heat for 5–7 minutes. Add the
mushrooms, carrots and celery and cook for a further
7–10 minutes.

3. Add the rosemary, thyme, sage, shoyu and black pepper.
Mix the mashed chestnuts in with the herbs. Pour in up to
$1/2$ pint (300ml) of the reserved chestnut stock to make a
moist mixture.

4. Put the chestnut mixture into a casserole or ovenproof dish.
Bake in a preheated oven at Gas Mark 4, 350°F, 180°C for 40
minutes. Serve hot.

Illustrated opposite

Top: **Chestnut and mushroom bake** (*see above*); Bottom: **Spinach with walnuts** (*see p. 78*).

SPINACH WITH WALNUTS

INGREDIENTS

2 lb (1kg) fresh spinach
(or 1½ lb/750g frozen leaf spinach)
1 tbsp (15ml) sunflower oil
1 onion, finely chopped
½ tsp black pepper
½ tsp grated nutmeg
¼ pint (150ml) smetana or
natural yogurt
2oz (50g) wholemeal breadcrumbs
2oz (50g) walnuts, roughly chopped

•

NUTRITION PROFILE

This recipe is an excellent source of protein, fibre, Vitamins A, B₁, B₂, B₆, C and E, folic acid, calcium, magnesium, zinc, iron and copper.

• Per portion •
Carbohydrate: 13g
Protein: 17.3g **Fibre:** 27.4g
Fat: 12.2g **Calories:** 225

Spinach is rich in iron and has a wonderfully strong flavour. Here it is combined with smetana or yogurt for extra creaminess, topped with crisp walnuts and breadcrumbs, and garnished with walnut halves and parsley. You can use fresh or frozen spinach for this recipe, but fresh gives the best flavour.

Preparation time: 35 mins   Cooking time: 20 mins
Serves 4

METHOD

1. Wash the spinach if using fresh, in several changes of water. Put it into a large pan with a little extra water, cover tightly and cook gently over a low heat, stirring occasionally, for about 10 minutes until the spinach has reduced and is tender.

2. Drain in a colander and then chop. If using frozen spinach, cook according to the directions on the packet. Then drain in a colander, and chop.

3. Heat 2 tsp (10ml) of the oil in a large pan over a moderate heat and gently fry the onion for 10 minutes until soft.

4. Add the cooked spinach, black pepper and nutmeg and cook for 5 minutes.

5. Remove from the heat and stir in the smetana or yogurt. Put the spinach mixture into a casserole or ovenproof dish.

6. Mix together the breadcrumbs, chopped walnuts and the remaining 1 tsp (5ml) of oil. Sprinkle over the spinach.

7. Bake in a preheated oven at Gas Mark 4, 350°F, 180°C for 20 minutes. Serve hot garnished with walnut halves and fresh parsley.

Illustrated on page 77

TURNIPS AND PEARS
WITH HERBS

INGREDIENTS

2 small turnips, thinly sliced in rings
2 pears, cored and thinly sliced in rings
$^1/_2$ tsp chopped fresh marjoram
$^1/_2$ tsp chopped fresh basil
$^1/_4$ tsp black pepper
$^1/_4$ pint (150ml) water
1 tsp (5ml) concentrated apple juice
$^1/_2$ tsp cider vinegar
2 tsp (10ml) arrowroot

•

NUTRITION PROFILE

*This low-calorie, low-fat recipe is a good
source of Vitamin C.*

• Per portion •
Carbohydrate: 8g
Protein: 0.6g **Fibre:** 2.6g
Fat: 0.2g **Calories:** 35

*The contrast between the flavour and texture of the turnips and pears
makes this a good accompaniment to a fairly plain main course.*

Preparation time: 10 mins   Cooking time: 1$^1/_2$ hours
Serves 4

METHOD

1. Layer the turnips and pears in a large casserole or ovenproof
dish and sprinkle with marjoram, basil and black pepper.

2. Mix the water, apple juice and cider vinegar. Pour over the
turnips and pears. Cover the casserole and bake in a preheated
oven at Gas Mark 4, 350°F, 180°C for 1$^1/_2$ hours.

3. Drain off the stock from the casserole. Mix a little of it with the
arrowroot to make a thick paste. Gradually add the rest.

4. Transfer to a small pan and bring to the boil, stirring
continuously, until the sauce becomes thick and clear. Pour over
the turnips and pears and serve hot.

Illustrated on page 80

CELERIAC WITH CASHEWS

INGREDIENTS

1 lb (500g) celeriac, chopped
1 lb (500g) potatoes, chopped
4 tbsp (60ml) natural yogurt
3 tbsp (45ml) chopped fresh parsley
$^1/_4$ tsp black pepper
3oz (75g) unsalted cashew nuts

•

NUTRITION PROFILE

*A good source of fibre, this dish also
contains Vitamins B$_1$, B$_6$ and C,
calcium, iron and magnesium.*

• Per portion •
Carbohydrate: 33.8g
Protein: 9g **Fibre:** 9.7g
Fat: 8.9g **Calories:** 240

*A purée of celeriac and potato, combined here with cashew nuts, makes
a nutritious accompaniment to a bean or vegetable casserole. If celeriac
is not available, try using swede instead.*

Preparation time: 25 mins   Cooking time: 25 mins
Serves 4

METHOD

1. Put the celeriac and potatoes into a large pan. Cover with
plenty of water and bring to the boil. Simmer gently for 10–15
minutes until the vegetables are cooked. Drain and mash well.

2. Stir in the yogurt, parsley, pepper and most of the cashew nuts.
Put into a casserole or ovenproof dish and sprinkle the rest of the
cashew nuts on top.

3. Bake in a preheated oven at Gas Mark 4, 350°F, 180°C for 25
minutes until the cashew nuts become golden brown.

Illustrated on page 80

CIDER CASSEROLE

INGREDIENTS

1 lb (500g) potatoes, cut into ¼ inch (5mm) slices
1 onion, finely sliced into rings
8oz (250g) sharp eating apples, cored and sliced
3oz (75g) Cheddar cheese, grated
3 tbsp (45ml) chopped fresh parsley
¼ pint (150ml) dry cider

•

NUTRITION PROFILE

This casserole is rich in Vitamins A, B_6, B_{12} and C and calcium.

• Per portion •
Carbohydrate: 35.8g
Protein: 8.2g   Fibre: 4.7g
Fat: 6.4g   Calories: 230

This traditional combination of potatoes and apples is enhanced here by the addition of cider as the cooking stock. Serve this casserole as a simple lunch dish or as a vegetable accompaniment to a main course.

Preparation time: 15 mins   Cooking time: 1–1½ hours
Serves 4

METHOD

1. Layer the potatoes, onion, apples, most of the cheese and the parsley in a large casserole or ovenproof dish, reserving some of the cheese to sprinkle on the top.

2. Pour over the cider. Sprinkle on the rest of the cheese and cover.

3. Bake in a preheated oven at Gas Mark 5, 375°F, 190°C for 1–1½ hours until the potatoes are tender. Serve hot.

Illustrated opposite

SESAME FRUITS

INGREDIENTS

4 medium oranges, peeled and thinly sliced into rings
2 tart eating apples, cored and thinly sliced into rings
2 tbsp (30ml) tahini
2 tbsp (30ml) concentrated apple juice
¼ pint (150ml) water
1 tbsp (15ml) sesame seeds

•

NUTRITION PROFILE

This fruit dessert is rich in Vitamin C.

• Per portion •
Carbohydrate: 17.2g
Protein: 4.3g   Fibre: 3.3g
Fat: 6.9g   Calories: 140

Tahini, a sesame seed paste, is mixed with concentrated apple juice to make a good sweet or savoury sauce for a layer of thinly sliced oranges and apples. This can be served as a dessert or as an accompaniment to a rich savoury dish like a roast or loaf.

Preparation time: 10 mins   Cooking time: 30 mins
Serves 4

METHOD

1. Layer the orange and apple slices in a casserole or ovenproof dish.

2. Mix together the tahini and apple juice to form a smooth paste. Add the water gradually, stirring to form a smooth sauce. Pour over the fruits.

3. Sprinkle over the sesame seeds. Cover the casserole or dish.

4. Bake in a preheated oven at Gas Mark 4, 350°F, 180°C for 30 minutes. Serve hot or cold.

Illustrated on page 83

Clockwise from top left: **Turnips and pears with herbs** (see p.79); **Celeriac with cashews** (see p.79); **Cider casserole** (see above).

SPICED NECTARINES

INGREDIENTS

4 nectarines, halved and stoned
½ pint (300ml) apple juice (or 3 tbsp/
45ml concentrated apple juice and
½ pint/300ml water)
1 tsp (5ml) ground cinnamon
½ tsp grated nutmeg
2 cloves
2oz (50g) bulgar wheat

•

NUTRITION PROFILE

*Low in fat and calories, this dessert
contains a useful amount of Vitamins
A and C.*

• Per portion •
Carbohydrate: 27.4g
Protein: 2.2g **Fibre:** 2.6g
Fat: 0.3g **Calories:** 125

*Nectarines, peaches or plums cooked gently in spices and apple juice,
with no added sugar, are delicious hot or cold with Greek strained
yogurt. If nectarines are unavailable, try using apples or pears instead.
Concentrated apple juice gives added sweetness and bulgar wheat helps
to thicken the sauce.*

Preparation time: 10 mins   Cooking time: 10 mins
Serves 4

METHOD

1. Put the nectarines, apple juice (or concentrated apple juice
and water), cinnamon, nutmeg, cloves and bulgar wheat into a
large pan. Bring to the boil, reduce the heat and simmer gently
for 10 minutes, until the fruit is just soft.

2. Discard the cloves. Serve hot or cold.

Illustrated opposite

CRISP PEACHES

INGREDIENTS

4 peaches
3oz (75g) hazelnuts, coarsely ground
1 tbsp (15ml) ground cinnamon
1 tbsp (15ml) clear honey
1oz (25g) vegetable margarine
3–4 tbsp (45–60ml) water

•

NUTRITION PROFILE

*This dessert is rich in Vitamins A, C,
D and E.*

• Per portion •
Carbohydrate: 16.5g
Protein: 2.2g **Fibre:** 2.6g
Fat: 12g **Calories:** 180

*Served hot or cold with natural yogurt, smetana or fromage frais, this
versatile recipe makes a healthy, yet luxurious dessert. Hazelnuts,
relatively low in fat and calories, are used in the topping with honey to
sweeten. Pears could be used when peaches are unavailable.*

Preparation time: 15 mins   Cooking time: 20–25 mins
Serves 4

METHOD

1. Halve and stone the peaches. Put into the base of a large
casserole or ovenproof dish with the cut sides uppermost.

2. Combine the hazelnuts and cinnamon in a small bowl. Melt
the honey and margarine over a moderate heat in a small pan.
Pour over the hazelnuts and cinnamon and mix well.

3. Top each of the peach halves with some of the nut mixture.
Spoon the water around the peaches and cover the dish.

4. Bake in a preheated oven at Gas Mark 4, 350°F, 180°C for 20
minutes. If desired, the peaches can be browned under a
preheated moderate grill for 5 minutes before serving. Serve
hot or cold.

Illustrated opposite

From top: **Sesame fruits** (*see p. 81*); **Crisp peaches** (*see above*); **Spiced nectarines** (*see above*).

MILLET AND PEAR PUDDING

INGREDIENTS

1 tsp (5ml) sunflower oil
3oz (75g) millet
¾ pint (450ml) skimmed milk
3 tbsp (45ml) concentrated apple juice
1oz (25g) sultanas
1 tsp (5ml) ground cinnamon
1 egg, separated
4 ripe pears, cored and sliced
1oz (25g) flaked almonds, toasted

•

NUTRITION PROFILE

This pudding is a good source of Vitamins B_2, B_{12}, C and E and calcium.

• Per portion •
Carbohydrate: 38.3g
Protein: 7.9g **Fibre:** 4.4g
Fat: 8.1g **Calories:** 255

Millet, which is rich in protein, calcium and iron, makes a light, fluffy topping over fresh pear slices. Other fruits – pineapple and bananas or peaches and oranges, for example – would work equally well. Serve hot or cold, topped with a little yogurt.

Preparation time: 40 mins   Cooking time: 40 mins
Serves 4–6

METHOD

1. Heat the oil in a large pan and gently toast the millet over a moderate heat for 5 minutes, taking care not to
let it burn.

2. Add the milk, apple juice, sultanas and cinnamon. Bring to the boil, cover and simmer for 20 minutes; stir occasionally to prevent it from burning. When the millet is soft and fluffy, set aside to cool slightly.

3. Stir the egg yolk into the cooled millet. In a separate bowl, whisk the egg white until stiff, then gently fold into the millet mixture.

4. Lightly oil a 1 lb (500g) loaf tin or a small, deep, ovenproof dish. Put half of the pear slices and half of the flaked almonds into the base of the tin. Cover with half of the millet mixture. Then put in the rest of the pears and almonds. Top with the remaining millet.

5. Bake in a preheated oven at Gas Mark 4, 350°F, 180°C for 30–40 minutes until golden brown and firm to touch. Leave in the tin for a few minutes before turning out. Garnish this pudding with pear slices, grapes and mint, and serve hot or cold.

Illustrated on page 86

HOT FRUIT SALAD

INGREDIENTS
1 tsp (5ml) sunflower oil
2 dessert apples, cut into eighths
2 peaches, cut into quarters
1 orange, peeled and segmented
4 plums, halved and stoned
1 banana, peeled and cut into chunks
1 tsp (5ml) ground cinnamon
1 tsp (5ml) clear honey

•

NUTRITION PROFILE

This low-fat, low-calorie dessert is a good source of Vitamin C.

• Per portion •
Carbohydrate: 21.8g
Protein: 1.1g **Fibre:** 3.2g
Fat: 1.4g **Calories:** 100

Low in calories, light and easy to make, this dessert is especially good when served with yogurt or smetana. The fruits can be varied according to availability, working on the basis of 1–2 fruits per person. Melon, grapes, greengages and pears are all good substitutes.

Preparation time: 10 mins   Cooking time: 8 mins
Serves 4

METHOD

1. Heat the oil in a large frying pan, saucepan or wok over a moderate heat. Add the apples and cook gently for 2–3 minutes.

2. Gradually add the peaches, orange and plums, cooking gently for 1 minute between each addition.

3. Finally add the banana and cinnamon and cook for 2 minutes. Drip the honey over the top. Serve hot or cold.

Illustrated on page 86

STIR-FRYING

Stir-frying is a Chinese technique for cooking vegetables in which a little oil is heated in a pan, preferably a wok (a thin round-bottomed metal pan which conducts heat well); the food is then cooked so that it retains its crispness, flavour and the maximum nutrients. Although we are familiar with the idea of stir-frying vegetables, fish and meat, it is perhaps surprising to learn that you can also stir-fry fruit. The same principles apply: use a little oil, add the slower cooking ingredients first, cook quickly and keep the ingredients moving.

1. Heat the oil, then add the hard-fleshed fruit, leaving 1 minute between each type of fruit.

2. Gradually add the soft-fleshed fruit, ending with the softest, leaving 1 minute between each.

3. When all the fruit has been added, stir for 2 minutes. Add any seasoning as directed in the recipe you are using (see above) and serve.

CASTLE FRUIT PUDDING

INGREDIENTS

6oz (175g) dried apricots (preferably
Hunzas), soaked
2 eating apples, sliced
½ pint (300ml) water
4oz (125g) porridge oats
4oz (125g) wholemeal flour
2oz (50g) raisins
2oz (50g) almonds, finely chopped
1oz (25g) sesame seeds
2 tsp (10ml) ground cinnamon
3oz (75g) vegetable margarine
3 tbsp (45ml) concentrated apple juice

TOPPING
2 tsp (10ml) sesame seeds

•
NUTRITION PROFILE

*This recipe is a good source of Vitamins A,
B, D and E and niacin, folic acid,
calcium, magnesium, iron and zinc.*

• Per portion •
Carbohydrate: 54.2g
Protein: 9.9g **Fibre:** 13.1g
Fat: 20g **Calories:** 420

*This crunchy baked pudding has a juicy layer of apricots and apples in
the middle. Dried fruits are naturally sweet, so this recipe does not need
added sugar. Dried fruits are also a good source of minerals and fibre.
Other combinations could be used, such as dried dates and fresh pears,
dried peaches and fresh bananas, dried figs and fresh oranges. This
pudding could also be served as a cake, cut into slices.*

Preparation time: 40 mins (plus overnight soaking time) Cooking time: 40 mins
Serves 6–8

METHOD

1. Put the apricots and apples into a medium pan and cover with
the water. Bring to the boil, cover and simmer for 15–20 minutes
until the apricots are soft. Add a little extra water during cooking
if the fruit seems dry.

2. When cooked, remove the stones from the apricots, if using
Hunzas. Mix well with a spoon to break them up slightly. Set
aside to cool.

3. Mix the oats, flour, raisins, almonds, sesame seeds and
cinnamon together in a large bowl. Melt the margarine in a small
pan. Pour over the oats and flour mixture. Add the concentrated
apple juice and mix well.

4. Press half the oat mixture into the base of a 7 inch (18cm)
round loose-bottomed tin. Cover with the apricots and apples.
Spoon over the rest of the oat mixture, pressing down well.
Sprinkle with the additional sesame seeds.

5. Bake in a preheated oven at Gas Mark 4, 350°F, 180°C for
35–40 minutes. Allow to stand in the tin for 5 minutes before
serving. Serve hot or cold.

Illustrated opposite

Clockwise from top right: **Millet and pear pudding** (*see p.84*); **Castle fruit pudding** (*see above*); **Hot fruit salad** (*see p. 85*).

FRUIT RISOTTO

INGREDIENTS

8oz (250g) long-grain brown rice
1 pint (600ml) skimmed milk
2 tbsp (30ml) concentrated apple juice
4oz (125g) black grapes, deseeded
1 peach, pear or nectarine, sliced
1 dessert apple, cored and sliced
1 banana, peeled and sliced
1 orange, peeled and cut into segments
4oz (125g) melon or pineapple, cubed
1oz (25g) flaked almonds, toasted
$\frac{1}{2}$ tsp ground cinnamon

•

NUTRITION PROFILE

This recipe provides Vitamins B_1, B_2, B_{12} and C, niacin, folic acid, calcium, magnesium, copper and zinc.

• Per portion •
Carbohydrate: 79.6g
Protein: 11.4g **Fibre:** 5.8g
Fat: 5.4g **Calories:** 390

This recipe makes a substantial dessert, sweetened only by the fruits and concentrated apple juice. Various fruits could be used with the rice according to availability. Serve topped with a little Greek strained yogurt and garnished with slices of orange.

Preparation time: 10 mins (plus cooling time)
Cooking time: 40 mins
Serves 4

METHOD

1. Put the rice, milk and apple juice into a large pan. Bring to the boil, cover and simmer gently for 30–40 minutes.

2. Remove from the heat and stir in the grapes, peach, pear or nectarine, apple, banana, orange and melon or pineapple. Set aside to cool.

3. When cool, put the risotto into one large or four individual dishes. Sprinkle with flaked almonds and the cinnamon.

Illustrated opposite

BANANA SURPRISE

INGREDIENTS

4 medium bananas
4 tbsp (60ml) fresh lemon juice
2oz (50g) flaked almonds
10oz (300g) silken tofu (or
$\frac{1}{2}$ pint/300ml natural yogurt)
2 tbsp (30ml) concentrated apple juice

•

NUTRITION PROFILE

This pudding is a good source of copper, calcium, magnesium, Vitamins B_6, C and E.

• Per portion •
Carbohydrate: 22.5g
Protein: 6.8g **Fibre:** 3.8g
Fat: 9g **Calories:** 200

Silken tofu, made from soya beans, makes a delicious low-fat, high-protein alternative to cream. It tastes equally good served with hot or cold fruit.

Preparation time: 20 mins   Cooking time: 20 mins
Serves 4

METHOD

1. Peel the bananas and slice into 1 inch (2.5cm) chunks. Put into a casserole or ovenproof dish and pour over the lemon juice.

2. Toast the almonds lightly under a preheated moderate grill for 5–10 minutes. Add to the banana. Cover and bake in a preheated oven at Gas Mark 4, 350°F, 180°C for 15 minutes.

3. Meanwhile, mix the tofu or yogurt with the concentrated apple juice. Do this in a blender or food processor if using tofu.

4. Pour the tofu or yogurt over the bananas. Serve straightaway garnished with lemon slices.

Illustrated opposite

Top: **Banana surprise** (*see above*); Bottom: **Fruit risotto** (*see above*).

NUTRITION CHARTS

The evidence that diet and disease are linked continues to mount. Eating a well-balanced diet can help to keep you in good health, or even improve your health. Medical conditions prevalent in today's society, including heart disease, diabetes, cancer of the bowel and even minor ailments like migraines can be wholly or partially eradicated by changing the foods we eat. In 1983, The National Advisory Committee on Nutrition Education produced a report on the links between diet and health. The following pages translate the recommendations into a palatable formula for a healthy diet. There is no need to forego our favourite foods in an effort to improve our diet; it is largely a question of re-thinking the quality and the type of food we eat and getting the balance right.

USING THE NUTRITION PROFILES

Our diet is made up of three major nutrients: proteins, fats and carbohydrates (including fibre, starch and sugar), each of which contributes to our calorie intake. But how much of each should we eat every day and which foods contain them? The charts (below) give our recommended daily intakes and list the foods richest in each nutrient. This information will in turn help you to use the nutrition profiles given with each recipe, to plan a balanced day's eating. A recipe that contains 15g of fibre, provides half your daily requirement of 30g per day.

CARBOHYDRATE

Carbohydrates, which are made up of sugars, starch and fibre, are the major source of energy in the diet. Excess is stored as fat. Unrefined carbohydrates are more nutritious than refined. Unrefined starches are richer in vitamins, help to maintain a steady blood sugar level and are lower in calories.
ADVICE: Eat more unrefined carbohydrates (wholemeal grains, bread and pasta, fresh fruit and vegetables and pulses).

Rich Sources of Carbohydrate

Recommended daily intake: 250–375g†

Split peas	1oz (25g) dry weight	Contains	71g
Lentils	1oz (25g) dry weight	..	67g
Potato	7oz (200g) baked	..	41g
Banana	1 (6oz/175g)	..	34g
Dried dates	2oz (50g)	..	32g
Wholemeal bread	2 slices (2½oz/70g)	..	29g
Dried prunes	2oz (50g)	..	20g
Black grapes	4oz (125g)	..	19g
Brown rice	2oz (50g) dry weight	..	16g
Beetroot	4oz (125g) cooked	..	12g

FIBRE

High-fibre foods help to keep the digestive system in good working order and in some cases lower cholesterol levels.
ADVICE: Eat more fibre (fresh and dried fruit and vegetables, wholegrains and pulses).

Rich Sources of Fibre

Recommended daily intake: 25–30g†

Dried apricots	2oz (50g)	Contains	12g
Peas	4oz (125g) fresh or frozen	..	11g
Blackcurrants	4oz (125g) stewed, no sugar	..	11g
Figs	2oz (50g) about 3 figs	..	9g
Raspberries	4oz (125g)	..	9g
Haricot beans	4oz (125g) cooked	..	9g
Spinach	4oz (125g) cooked	..	8g
Prunes	2oz (50g) dry weight	..	8g
Almonds	2oz (50g) shelled	..	7g
Butter beans	4oz (125g) cooked	..	6g
Wholemeal bread	2 slices (2½oz/70g)	..	6g
Potato	7oz (200g) baked	..	5g

PROTEIN

Protein is needed for growth and for the maintenance of healthy muscles and tissue. Vegetables and dairy products contain different forms of protein and by eating a wide range of food combinations, such as muesli with milk, pasta with cheese or beans with rice you can obtain complete, high-quality proteins.
ADVICE: Obtain main protein requirements from vegetable-based foods (grains, cereals, pulses).

Rich Sources of Protein

Recommended daily intake: 53–90g (men) 48–68g (women)†

Amounts expressed in typical portions

Soya flour	2oz (50g)	Contains	18g
Cottage cheese	4oz (125g) carton	..	17g
Cheddar cheese	2oz (50g)	..	13g
Peanuts	2oz (50g) shelled	..	12g
Skimmed milk	½ pint (300ml)	..	10g
Cashew nuts	2oz (50g)	..	9g
Egg	1 egg, size 3	..	6g
Wholemeal bread	2 slices (2 ½oz/70g)	..	6g
Potato	7oz (200g) baked	..	5g

† As recommended in Great Britain by the Department of Health and Social Security

FATS

There are three sources of fat: saturated, monounsaturated and polyunsaturated. Each of the three types are present in fatty foods in varying proportions. Saturated fats increase blood cholesterol levels, which can lead to heart disease. Polyunsaturated fats help to lower cholesterol levels.

ADVICE: Eat less fat. Within your daily allowance, include less saturated and more polyunsaturated fat (vegetable oils, nuts).

Sources of Polyunsaturated Fat

Recommended daily intake: 77–117g (about 35% of daily calories, of which only 15% (33–50g) should be saturated).†

Walnuts	2oz (50g)	*Contains* 26gF	*incl.* 18gPUF
Polyunsaturated margarine	1oz (25g)	..	20gF	..	15gPUF
Brazil nuts	2oz (50g)	..	31gF	..	12gPUF
Soya bean oil	1 tbsp (15ml)	..	12gF	..	7gPUF
Sunflower seed oil	1 tbsp (15ml)	..	12gF	..	6gPUF
Oatmeal	2tbsp (1oz/25g)	..	2gF	..	1gPUF

CALORIES

Almost everything we eat is turned into energy, which is measured in calories (sometimes called kilocalories), and used up by the body in activity and in keeping the body working. Calorie needs depend on sex, age, weight and activity, but if calorie intake constantly outstrips demand, body weight increases.

Calorie values

Recommended daily intake: Men 3,000 cals Women 2,200 cals†

Foods high in calories

Nuts	2oz (50g) almonds	*Contains*	285
	peanuts	..	285
	walnuts	..	265
Cheddar cheese	2oz (50g)	..	230
Avocado pear	½ (3½oz/100g) flesh	..	205
Butter/margarine	¾oz (20g)	..	185
Pastry	1½oz (40g)	..	165

Foods with average calories

Brown rice	2oz (50g) dry weight	..	180
Potato	7oz (200g) baked	..	175
Wholemeal pasta	2oz (50g) dry weight	..	160
Wholemeal bread	2 slices (2½oz/70g)	..	150
Soft curd cheese	2oz (50g)	..	95
Butterbeans	1oz (25g) dry weight	..	70
Mung beans	1oz (25g) dry weight	..	60

Foods low in calories

Cottage cheese	4oz (125g)	..	110
Skimmed milk	½ pint (300ml)	..	100
Yogurt	5oz (150g) natural	..	80
Fresh fruit	1 apple/orange	..	50
Low-fat soft cheese	2oz (50g)	..	40
Vegetables	4oz (125g) leeks	..	30
	4oz (125g) mushrooms	..	15

PLANNING BALANCED MEALS

It is easy to get the right amounts of carbohydrates, protein, fibre, fat, calories and the various vitamins and minerals from a vegetarian diet if you follow a few basic guidelines.

• Try to have three evenly sized meals a day. This keeps the blood sugar level steady and avoids taxing the digestive system and internal organs.

• If you have to eat between meals, have some fresh or dried fruit; crisp, raw vegetables; a piece of toast, sweetened with dried fruit or honey; or some nuts.

• Try to have one grain-based meal a day, such as toast for breakfast and rice or pasta at a main meal.

• Try to have at least one salad-based meal a day.

• Have one meal based on vegetarian protein (cheese, beans, nuts) each day and, if you are not vegetarian, limit animal protein (fish, eggs, meat) to about 3 times a week.

• Finish meals with fresh, stewed or dried fruit in place of high-fat, high-sugar desserts, such as cakes, pastries, ice creams.

• Try to limit tea or coffee to no more than 5 cups a day (or drink herbal tea and cereal coffee). Keep alcohol intake down to 2 glasses of wine or 1 pint of beer or cider a day.

SUGGESTIONS FOR DAILY PORTIONS

In an average day it is easy to eat too much of one sort of food and not enough of another. The chart (below) suggests how many portions of each type of food you should aim to eat with limited examples of how to obtain them.

NUMBER OF PORTIONS	FOOD	EXAMPLES
4	Dairy	1 cup skimmed milk • 5oz (150g) natural yogurt • 1oz (25g) cheese • 1 egg
4	Vegetables	4oz (125g) spinach • 4oz (125g) carrots • 4oz (125g) broccoli
3	Fruits	Glass unsweetened orange juice • 1 apple or orange • 2oz (50g) dried prunes
4	Grains	2 slices wholemeal bread • 4oz (125g) brown rice • 2oz (50g) pasta
4	Beans and nuts	2oz (50g) cashew nuts • 2oz (50g) sesame seeds • 4oz (125g) cooked beans

VITAMINS

Alcohol, the contraceptive pill, caffeine, smoking and food processing slows the absorption of some vitamins, so raising daily needs. Vegetarians should check their Vitamin B_{12} intake. (1,000mg = 1g 1,000µg = 1mg).

VITAMIN	USES	DAILY INTAKE†	RICH VEGETARIAN SOURCES
A	Promotes night vision, healthy eyes, skin, hair, nails and internal mucous membranes. Helps the utilization of fat and Vitamin C and the action of the liver and thyroid.	750µg*	4oz (125g) watercress: 3,750µg • 4oz (125g) carrots: 2,500µg • 4oz (125g) cooked spinach: 1,250µg • 2oz (50g) dried apricots: 300µg • 4oz (125g) broccoli: 521µg • ½ pint (300ml) whole milk: 116µg • 1 medium tomato (3oz/75g): 75µg • 1 egg (2oz/50g): 70µg
B_1 (thiamin)	Helps to metabolize carbohydrate. Keeps the nervous system, brain, muscles, and heart functioning well. Some losses with cooking.	1.2mg	2 slices wholemeal bread (2½oz/70g): 0.2mg • 2oz (50g) brazil nuts: 0.5mg • 2oz (50g) peanuts: 0.5mg • 4oz (125g) cooked peas: 0.3mg • 3tsp (¼oz/7g) yeast extract: 0.2mg • 1 tbsp (¼oz/7g) wheatgerm: 0.1mg
B_2 (riboflavin)	Keeps skin, eyes, nails, hair and lips healthy. With thiamin, helps to metabolize carbohydrates. Helps thyroid function.	1.6mg**	½ pint (300ml) skimmed milk: 0.6mg • 4oz (125g) mushrooms: 0.5mg • 2oz (50g) almonds: 0.5mg • 5oz (150ml) natural yogurt: 0.4mg • 2oz (50g) Cheddar cheese: 0.3mg • 1 egg (2oz/50g): 0.2mg
Niacin (Vitamin B_3)	Keeps brain and nervous system functioning well. Helps to metabolize food and to synthesize hormones.	18mg**	2oz (50g) peanuts: 8mg • 3 tsp (¼oz/7g) yeast extract: 4mg • 4oz (125g) mushrooms: 5mg • 4oz (125g) cooked broad beans: 4mg • 2oz (50g) dried peaches: 3mg • 2 slices wholemeal bread (2½oz/70g): 3mg
B_6	Helps the body to use protein, fats and iron. Important in nerve, brain, blood and muscle functioning. Controls cholesterol levels. Activates enzymes.	No official guideline but 1.5–2mg advised**	1 tbsp (⅛oz/3.5g) bran: 0.04mg • 1 tbsp (¼oz/7g) wheatgerm: 0.07mg • 3 tsp (¼oz/7g) yeast extract: 0.09mg • 2 tbsp (1oz/25g) oatmeal: 0.15mg • 2oz (50g) walnuts: 0.37mg • 2oz (50g) soya flour: 0.28mg • 2oz (50g) hazelnuts: 0.28mg • 1 banana (5oz/150g): 0.77mg
B_{12}	Helps to form blood cells and metabolize food. Prevents pernicious anaemia. Works with folic acid. Vegetarians, especially vegans, may be deficient.	2µg	1 egg yolk (¾oz/20g): 0.98µg • 1 egg (2oz/50g): 0.85mg • 2oz (50g) Cheddar cheese: 0.75µg • 2oz (50g) Parmesan cheese: 0.75µg • 2oz (50g) Brie and low-fat soft cheeses: 0.6µg • 3 tsp (¼oz/7g) yeast extract: 0.04µg • 4oz (125g) carton cottage cheese: 0.63µg
Folic Acid	Helps form red blood cells, and genetic material, metabolize protein and sugars, and make antibodies. Promotes healthy skin and wards off anaemia.	400µg**	4oz (125g) cooked spinach: 175µg • 2oz (50g) raw endive: 165µg • 4oz (125g) cooked broccoli: 138µg • 4oz (125g) cooked Brussel sprouts: 109µg • 3 tsp (¼oz/7g) yeast extract: 71µg • 2oz (50g) peanuts: 55µg • 2oz (50g) almonds: 48µg • 1tbsp (¼oz/7g) wheatgerm: 23.1µg
C	Helps to prevent disease and infection, increases anti-bodies and energy levels. Aids calcium and oxygen metabolism, and iron absorption, lowers cholesterol.	30mg	1 red or green pepper (5oz/150g): 130mg • 4oz (125g) blackcurrants: 250mg • juice of 1 lemon: 80 mg • 4oz (125g) strawberries: 75mg • 4oz (125g) boiled spring cabbage: 31mg • 4oz (125g) boiled potatoes: 18mg • 3 sprigs parsley (¼oz/7g): 11mg • 4oz (125g) spinach: 6mg
D	Helps in absorption of calcium and phosphorus. Keeps heart, nervous system, eyes, bones and teeth healthy.	2.5µg***	¾oz (20g) margarine: 1.6µg • 1 egg yolk (¾oz/20g): 1.0µg • 2oz (50g) Cheddar: 0.1µg • 2oz (50g) Parmesan cheese: 0.1µg • ½ pint (300ml) whole milk: 0.1µg
E	Protects cell walls. Helps wounds to heal quickly. Relieves heart conditions. Stimulates immune system. Deficiency very rare.	No guideline in UK.	2oz (50g) hazelnuts: 10.5mg • 2oz (50g) almonds: 10mg • 1 tbsp (15ml) sunflower oil: 7.2mg • 2oz (50g) peanuts: 4.05mg • 2oz (50g) Brazil nuts: 3.25mg • ¾oz (20g) margarine: 1.6mg • 1 tbsp (¼oz/7g) wheatgerm: 0.8mg

† As recommended in Great Britain by the Department of Health and Social Security

MINERALS

A diet rich in vegetable-based foods should supply plenty of minerals. Pregnant women and growing children may need a little more, and alcohol, smoking, caffeine and the Pill can also increase daily needs.

MINERAL	USES	DAILY INTAKE†	RICH MINERAL SOURCES
Iron	Essential for the formation of haemoglobin and to carry oxygen. Vegans, vegetarians and children may be deficient.	Men: 10mg Women: 12mg**	1oz (25g) blackstrap molasses: 4mg ● 1 tbsp ($^1/_8$oz/3.5g) bran: 0.4mg ● 1 tbsp ($^1/_4$oz/7g) wheatgerm: 0.7mg ● 3 sprigs parsley ($^1/_4$oz/7g): 0.6mg ● 2oz (50g) soya flour: 3.5mg ● 2oz (50g) dried peaches: 3.4mg
Calcium	Works with Vitamin D to promote healthy bones, teeth and nerves. Deficiency can cause osteoporosis in older people.	500mg**	2oz (50g) Parmesan cheese: 610mg ● 2oz (50g) Cheddar cheese: 400mg ● 4oz (125g) cooked spinach: 750mg ● 2oz (50g) Brie and soft cheeses: 190mg ● 3 sprigs parsley ($^1/_4$oz/7g): 30mg ● 2oz (50g) dried figs: 140mg
Magnesium	Helps synthesis of protein and fats and use of calcium, potassium, sodium and Vitamin B$_6$. Maintains healthy heart beat.	No official guideline but 200–400mg advised	2oz (50g) brazil nuts: 205mg ● 2oz (50g) almonds: 130mg ● 2oz (50g) soya flour: 120mg ● 2oz (50g) peanuts: 90mg ● 2oz (50g) wholemeal flour: 70mg ● 2oz (50g) walnuts: 65mg ● 2 slices wholemeal bread (2$^1/_2$oz/70g): 65mg
Potassium	Acts with sodium to regulate the body fluids, maintain the acid/alkali balance and to transport nerve impulses to muscles. Dietary deficiency rare.	No official guidelines in UK	2oz (50g) dried apricots: 940mg ● 2oz (50g) soya flour: 830mg ● 1oz (25g) blackstrap molasses: 732mg ● 2oz (50g) dried peaches: 550mg ● 2oz (50g) dried figs: 505mg ● 2oz (50g) sultanas: 430mg ● 3 tsp ($^1/_4$oz/7g) yeast extract: 182mg ● 3 sprigs parsley ($^1/_4$oz/7g): 97mg
Zinc	Essential for enzyme action. Aids vision and bone growth. Zinc absorption is reduced by a high-fibre diet.	15mg	2oz (50g) brazil nuts: 2.1mg ● 2oz (50g) Parmesan cheese: 2mg ● 2oz (50g) Cheddar cheese: 2mg ● 2oz (50g) almonds: 1.6mg ● 2oz (50g) peanuts or walnuts: 1.5mg ● 2 slices wholemeal bread (2$^1/_2$oz/70g): 1.4mg

FINDING HEALTHIER ALTERNATIVES

Healthy eating does not have to be a deprivation. By simply replacing high-fat, high-sugar and high-salt foods with more nutritious alternatives, you can dramatically improve your diet. Here are some suggestions.

TYPICAL FOODS	GOOD ALTERNATIVES	TYPICAL FOODS	GOOD ALTERNATIVES
jam/marmalade	low-sugar, high-fruit preserves	full-fat hard cheeses	Edam or Gouda, or low-fat cheese
fruit stewed with sugar	fruit stewed with concentrated juice	meat	pulses, lentils, nuts, grains, pastas, tofu
fruit canned in syrup	fruit canned in natural juices	butter, hard margarine	polyunsaturated margarine
sweetened carbonated drinks	sparkling or natural fruit juices, still or sparkling mineral water	chips	jacket potatoes or boiled in skins
sugary snacks	fresh fruit or dried fruit	unspecified vegetable oil	oil high in polyunsaturates, e.g. safflower, sunflower, soya
sugar on cereals	fresh fruit or dried fruit	salt	herbs and spices, shoyu, gomashio
confectionery	fresh fruit, dried fruit or fruit bars	cream cakes	wholemeal fruit breads
salted cocktail snacks	unsalted nuts, raw vegetable strips	tea	herb teas
full-cream milk	fresh skimmed milk, soya milk	chocolate/cocoa	carob
cream, evaporated or condensed milk	natural yogurt, smetana, silken tofu, buttermilk or natural fromage frais	white bread	wholemeal, rye, flavoured bread
full-fat soft cheeses	skimmed milk soft cheese (quark), cottage cheese, ricotta, tofu or brie	fried vegetables	steamed, baked or raw vegetables
		lard	vegetable fat or oil

* Requirement increased in lactating women
* * Requirement increased in pregnant and lactating women
* * * Requirement increased in young children, pregnant and lactating women

INDEX

ACKNOWLEDGMENTS

EDITOR: Rosanne Hooper
ART EDITOR: Anita Ruddell
ASSISTANT EDITOR: Rebecca Abrams
DESIGNER: Sally Powell
EDITORIAL ASSISTANT: Sophie Galleymore-Bird

EDITORIAL DIRECTOR: Alan Buckingham
ART DIRECTOR: Stuart Jackman

PHOTOGRAPHER: Graeme Harris
HOME ECONOMIST: Anne Hildyard
STYLIST: Carolyn Russell
ILLUSTRATOR: Nancy Anderson

TYPESETTING: Tradespools, Frome
REPRODUCTION: Singapore
PRINTING: Arnoldo Mondadori, Verona, Italy

Author's acknowledgments
Christine Smith would like to thank Rob Parfitt for his lively
help and her friends and colleagues, particularly Sarah
Brown, for their encouragement, support and advice.

Dorling Kindersley would like to thank: Barbara Croxford for
her help with the recipes; Dr Michèle Sadler for her work on the
Nutrition profiles; Fred and Cathy Gill, Gill Aspery and Janice
Lacock for invaluable proof-reading; Judy Sandeman for
efficient production control; Hilary Bird for the index; The
Vegetarian Society and The Fresh Fruit and Vegetable
Information Bureau for their help; Everyday Gourmet, 229
Kensington Church Street, London W8, David Mellor and
Elizabeth David for props; Jimmy Tsao and Josephine for their
hardwork.